LEARN ESPERANTO IN 52 WEEKS

LEARN ESPERANTO IN 52 WEEKS
WITH 7 SENTENCES A DAY

All rights reserved. No part of this publication may be reproduced, distributed, or transmitted in any form or by any means, including photocopying, recording, or other electronic or mechanical methods, without the prior written permission of the publisher, except in the case of brief quotations embodied in critical reviews and certain other noncommercial uses permitted by copyright law.

In the same collection

Learn English in 52 weeks
Learn French in 52 weeks
Learn Bulgarian in 52 weeks
Learn Chinese in 52 weeks
Learn Czech in 52 weeks
Learn Danish in 52 weeks
Learn Dutch in 52 weeks
Learn Estonian in 52 weeks
Learn Finnish in 52 weeks
Learn German in 52 weeks
Learn Greek in 52 weeks
Learn Hungarian in 52 weeks
Learn Italian in 52 weeks
Learn Japanese in 52 weeks
Learn Latvian in 52 weeks
Learn Lithuanian in 52 weeks
Learn Polish in 52 weeks
Learn Portuguese in 52 weeks
Learn Brazilian in 52 weeks
Learn Romanian in 52 weeks
Learn Russian in 52 weeks
Learn Slovak in 52 weeks
Learn Spanish in 52 weeks
Learn Swedish in 52 weeks

Contents

Week 1	Day 1-7
Week 2	Day 8-14
Week 3	Day 15-21
Week 4	Day 22-28
Week 5	Day 29-35
Week 6	Day 36-42
Week 7	Day 43-49
Week 8	Day 50-56
Week 9	Day 57-63
Week 10	Day 64-70
Week 11	Day 71-77
Week 12	Day 78-84
Week 13	Day 85-91
Week 14	Day 92-98
Week 15	Day 99-105
Week 16	Day 106-112
Week 17	Day 113-119
Week 18	Day 120-126
Week 19	Day 127-133
Week 20	Day 134-140
Week 21	Day 141-147
Week 22	Day 148-154
Week 23	Day 155-161
Week 24	Day 162-168
Week 25	Day 169-175
Week 26	Day 176-182
Week 27	Day 183-189

Week 28	…………………………………	Day 190-196
Week 29	…………………………………	Day 197-203
Week 30	…………………………………	Day 204-210
Week 31	…………………………………	Day 211-217
Week 32	…………………………………	Day 218-224
Week 33	…………………………………	Day 225-231
Week 34	…………………………………	Day 232-238
Week 35	…………………………………	Day 239-245
Week 36	…………………………………	Day 246-252
Week 37	…………………………………	Day 253-259
Week 38	…………………………………	Day 260-266
Week 39	…………………………………	Day 267-273
Week 40	…………………………………	Day 274-280
Week 41	…………………………………	Day 281-287
Week 42	…………………………………	Day 288-294
Week 43	…………………………………	Day 295-301
Week 44	…………………………………	Day 302-308
Week 45	…………………………………	Day 309-315
Week 46	…………………………………	Day 316-322
Week 47	…………………………………	Day 323-329
Week 48	…………………………………	Day 330-336
Week 49	…………………………………	Day 337-343
Week 50	…………………………………	Day 344-350
Week 51	…………………………………	Day 351-357
Week 52	…………………………………	Day 358-364

LEARN ESPERANTO IN 52 WEEKS

LEARN ESPERANTO IN 52 WEEKS WITH 7 SENTENCES A DAY

Week 1

1 - 1

Is it good for me?
Ĉu ĝi estas bona por mi?

1 - 2

Read the paragraph.
Legu la alineon.

1 - 3

Don't cry.
Ne ploru.

1 - 4

Don't go there.
Ne iru tien.

1 - 5

Keep your word.
Konservu vian vorton.

1 - 6

Which one do you want?
Kiun vi volas?

1 - 7

She is nearsighted.
Ŝi estas miopa.

Day 1

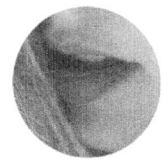

Week 1

2 - 1
The steak looks rare.
La bifsteko aspektas malofta.

2 - 2
I started a new job.
Mi komencis novan laboron.

2 - 3
The bag was sold out.
La sako estis elĉerpita.

2 - 4
Monitor your weight.
Monitoru vian pezon.

2 - 5
This is my fiancé.
Ĉi tiu estas mia fianĉo.

2 - 6
I ate heartily.
Mi manĝis kore.

2 - 7
Get dressed quickly.
Vestu vin rapide.

Day 2

LEARN ESPERANTO IN 52 WEEKS

LEARN ESPERANTO IN 52 WEEKS WITH 7 SENTENCES A DAY

Week 1

1/52

3 - 1

The water is hard.
La akvo estas malmola.

3 - 2

Do you do alterations?
Ĉu vi faras ŝanĝojn?

3 - 3

No problem.
Nedankinde.

3 - 4

The scenery is great.
La pejzaĝo estas bonega.

3 - 5

Please give me a hint.
Bonvolu doni al mi sugeston.

3 - 6

They have guns.
Ili havas pafilojn.

3 - 7

Who are you?
Kiu vi estas?

Day 3

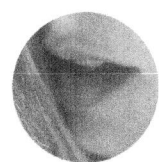

Week 1

4 - 1

His father is a teacher.
Lia patro estas instruisto.

4 - 2

I have a half-sister.
Mi havas duonfratinon.

4 - 3

No, i don't have one.
Ne, mi ne havas.

4 - 4

I have pain in my back.
Mi havas doloron en mia dorso.

4 - 5

It's was nothing.
Ĝi estis nenio.

4 - 6

Time flies.
Tempo flugas.

4 - 7

I am mary.
Mi estas maria.

Day 4

LEARN ESPERANTO IN 52 WEEKS

LEARN ESPERANTO IN 52 WEEKS WITH 7 SENTENCES A DAY

Week 1

5 - 1

Are you sure?
Ĉu vi certas?

5 - 2

I'm home.
Mi estas hejme.

5 - 3

I hate tests.
Mi malamas testojn.

5 - 4

Don't quarrel with him.
Ne kverelu kun li.

5 - 5

I'm on holiday.
Mi ferias.

5 - 6

Please bend your knees.
Bonvolu fleksi viajn genuojn.

5 - 7

He combed his hair.
Li kombis siajn harojn.

Day 5

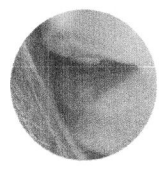

Week 1

6 - 1

Happy new year!
Feliĉan novjaron!

6 - 2

My foot went numb.
Mia piedo senkuraĝiĝis.

6 - 3

I rarely watch tv.
Mi malofte rigardas televidon.

6 - 4

Go straight on.
Iru rekte.

6 - 5

I want more freedom.
Mi volas pli da libereco.

6 - 6

I wish he gets well.
Mi deziras, ke li resaniĝos.

6 - 7

He always wears jeans.
Li ĉiam portas ĝinzon.

Day 6

LEARN ESPERANTO IN 52 WEEKS WITH 7 SENTENCES A DAY

Test 1

7 - 1

Which one do you want?

7 - 2

This is my fiancé.

7 - 3

The scenery is great.

7 - 4

No, i don't have one.

7 - 5

I'm home.

7 - 6

Happy new year!

7 - 7

He always wears jeans.

Day 7

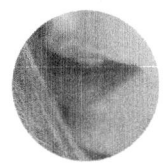

LEARN ESPERANTO IN 52 WEEKS
LEARN ESPERANTO IN 52 WEEKS WITH 7 SENTENCES A DAY

Week 2

8 - 1

I can't stop vomiting.
Mi ne povas ĉesi vomi.

8 - 2

Challenge yourself.
Defiu vin mem.

8 - 3

Excellent.
Bonega.

8 - 4

I injured my thumb.
Mi vundis mian dikfingron.

8 - 5

I can't avoid it.
Mi ne povas eviti ĝin.

8 - 6

There's a bomb!
Estas bombo!

8 - 7

Cross the street.
Transiru la straton.

Day 8

LEARN ESPERANTO IN 52 WEEKS
LEARN ESPERANTO IN 52 WEEKS WITH 7 SENTENCES A DAY

Week 2

9 - 1

I'm very sorry.
Mi tre bedaŭras.

9 - 2

How is life?
Kiel estas la vivo?

9 - 3

Can i take any message?
Ĉu mi povas preni iun mesaĝon?

9 - 4

She is my wife.
Ŝi estas mia edzino.

9 - 5

Please open the door.
Bonvolu malfermi la pordon.

9 - 6

She's a romantic person.
Ŝi estas romantika persono.

9 - 7

Please feel free.
Bonvolu senti vin libera.

Day 9

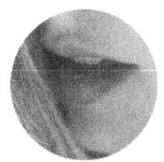

Week 2

10 - 1

I called the waitress.
Mi vokis la kelnerinon.

10 - 2

He hit on a good idea.
Li trafis bonan ideon.

10 - 3

Boys, be ambitious.
Knaboj, estu ambiciaj.

10 - 4

His story was funny.
Lia rakonto estis amuza.

10 - 5

Hide it up somewhere.
Kaŝu ĝin ie.

10 - 6

How are you feeling?
Kiel vi fartas?

10 - 7

She's a fashion expert.
Ŝi estas fakulo en modo.

Day 10

Week 2

11 - 1

It sounds good.
Ĝi sonas bone.

11 - 2

I have no choice.
Mi ne havas elekton.

11 - 3

Jump at the chance.
Saltu ĉe la ŝanco.

11 - 4

You're wrong.
Vi malpravas.

11 - 5

Time went by so fast.
La tempo pasis tiel rapide.

11 - 6

Is breakfast included?
Ĉu matenmanĝo estas inkluzivita?

11 - 7

Please come closer.
Bonvolu alproksimiĝi.

Day 11

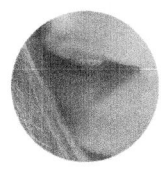

Week 2

12 - 1

This soup is very hot.
Ĉi tiu supo estas tre varma.

12 - 2

Your hair is still wet.
Via hararo ankoraŭ estas malseka.

12 - 3

What time is it?
Kioma horo estas?

12 - 4

What was your first job?
Kio estis via unua laboro?

12 - 5

Fasten your seat belt.
Buku vian sekur-zonon.

12 - 6

My son brought a friend.
Mia filo alportis amikon.

12 - 7

Take care.
Zorgu.

Day 12

Week 2

13 - 1
He's a soccer player.
Li estas futbalisto.

13 - 2
Fantastic.
Mirinda.

13 - 3
The battery is flat.
La baterio estas malbena.

13 - 4
How do you manage?
Kiel vi administras?

13 - 5
How do you go to office?
Kiel vi iras al oficejo?

13 - 6
It's a full moon today.
Estas plenluno hodiaŭ.

13 - 7
Insert your pin code.
Enigu vian pinkodon.

Day 13

Test 2

14 - 1

There's a bomb!

14 - 2

Please open the door.

14 - 3

His story was funny.

14 - 4

Jump at the chance.

14 - 5

Your hair is still wet.

14 - 6

He's a soccer player.

14 - 7

Insert your pin code.

Day 14

Week 3

15 - 1
I am fine.
Mi fartas bone.

15 - 2
Heat the pan.
Varmigu la paton.

15 - 3
Let's go by bus.
Ni iru per buso.

15 - 4
I feel shy.
Mi sentas min timema.

15 - 5
What did he say?
Kion li diris?

15 - 6
My trousers got dirty.
Mia pantalono malpuriĝis.

15 - 7
It's almost time.
Estas preskaŭ tempo.

Day 15

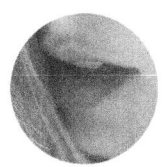

Week 3

16 - 1

My husband is out now.
Mia edzo estas ekstere nun.

16 - 2

The rear seat is empty.
La malantaŭa sidloko estas malplena.

16 - 3

She is a youth icon.
Ŝi estas junulara ikono.

16 - 4

He was greatly pleased.
Li estis tre kontenta.

16 - 5

Is the story true?
Ĉu la rakonto estas vera?

16 - 6

He is a lucky man.
Li estas bonŝanculo.

16 - 7

See you at 8 p.m.
Ĝis revido je la 20a.

Day 16

Week 3

17 - 1

He had indigestion.
Li havis indigeston.

17 - 2

Can you lift this table?
Ĉu vi povas levi ĉi tiun tablon?

17 - 3

Which bus shall i take?
Kiun buson mi prenu?

17 - 4

How long will you stay?
Kiom longe vi restos?

17 - 5

I accepted his opinion.
Mi akceptis lian opinion.

17 - 6

What's that?
Kio estas tio?

17 - 7

Please think carefully.
Bonvolu pripensi zorge.

Day 17

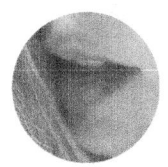

Week 3

18 - 1

Where do you work out?
Kie vi ekzercas?

18 - 2

I miss you.
Vi mankas al mi.

18 - 3

I think it's boring.
Mi pensas, ke ĝi estas enuiga.

18 - 4

Dry flat in shade.
Seka plata en ombro.

18 - 5

Don't be late.
Ne malfruu.

18 - 6

The bus is leaving.
La buso foriras.

18 - 7

Repeat after me.
Ripetu post mi.

Day 18

Week 3

19 - 1

I live with my friends.
Mi loĝas kun miaj amikoj.

19 - 2

Please pay in cash.
Bonvolu pagi kontante.

19 - 3

The sky's gray today.
La ĉielo estas griza hodiaŭ.

19 - 4

Happy birthday!
Feliĉan naskiĝtagon!

19 - 5

I was kidnapped.
Mi estis forrabita.

19 - 6

Do i have to do it now?
Ĉu mi devas fari ĝin nun?

19 - 7

You were almost right.
Vi preskaŭ pravis.

Day 19

Week 3

20 - 1

His house is very big.
Lia domo estas tre granda.

20 - 2

I saw the trailer.
Mi vidis la antaŭfilmon.

20 - 3

Yes, sunday is fine.
Jes, dimanĉo estas bone.

20 - 4

I see what you mean.
Mi komprenas, kion vi volas diri.

20 - 5

He stood on stage.
Li staris sur la scenejo.

20 - 6

I like dogs.
Mi ŝatas hundojn.

20 - 7

Would you like a bag?
Ĉu vi ŝatus sakon?

Day 20

Test 3

21 - 1

My trousers got dirty.

21 - 2

Is the story true?

21 - 3

How long will you stay?

21 - 4

I think it's boring.

21 - 5

Please pay in cash.

21 - 6

His house is very big.

21 - 7

Would you like a bag?

Day 21

Week 4

22 - 1

Can you show me how to?
Ĉu vi povas montri al mi kiel?

4/52

22 - 2

Thanks.
Dankon.

22 - 3

This box is heavy.
Ĉi tiu skatolo estas peza.

22 - 4

Where is the pilot?
Kie estas la piloto?

22 - 5

Turn headlights on.
Enŝaltu la lumojn.

22 - 6

The water is soft.
La akvo estas mola.

22 - 7

She's in the movie.
Ŝi estas en la filmo.

Day 22

Week 4

23 - 1
This dish is delicious.
Ĉi tiu plado estas bongusta.

23 - 2
I have lost my card.
Mi perdis mian karton.

23 - 3
Sure. just a moment.
Certe. nur momenton.

23 - 4
He has gone out.
Li eliris.

23 - 5
Did i ask them to wait?
Ĉu mi petis ilin atendi?

23 - 6
Put on your shirt.
Surmetu vian ĉemizon.

23 - 7
It's too big for me.
Ĝi estas tro granda por mi.

Day 23

LEARN ESPERANTO IN 52 WEEKS
LEARN ESPERANTO IN 52 WEEKS WITH 7 SENTENCES A DAY

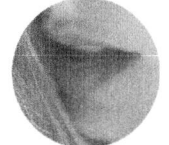

Week 4

24 - 1
Many thanks.
Dankegon.

24 - 2
It's been a long time.
Pasis longa tempo.

24 - 3
I need a doctor.
Mi bezonas kuraciston.

24 - 4
It's too short for me.
Ĝi estas tro mallonga por mi.

24 - 5
I have a student visa.
Mi havas studentan vizon.

24 - 6
Is she reading a novel?
Ĉu ŝi legas romanon?

24 - 7
Follow this road.
Sekvu ĉi tiun vojon.

Day 24

LEARN ESPERANTO IN 52 WEEKS
LEARN ESPERANTO IN 52 WEEKS WITH 7 SENTENCES A DAY

Week 4

25 - 1

I have no other choice.
Mi ne havas alian elekton.

25 - 2

How do you know that?
Kiel vi scias tion?

25 - 3

Please come at once.
Bonvolu veni tuj.

25 - 4

Glad to meet you.
Ĝojas renkonti vin.

25 - 5

My camera broke.
Mia fotilo rompiĝis.

25 - 6

I know that.
Mi scias tion.

25 - 7

Was i appointed?
Ĉu mi estis nomumita?

Day 25

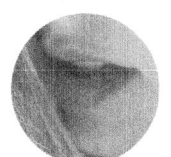

Week 4

26 - 1

How much is it?
Kiom kostas tio?

26 - 2

He is smart.
Li estas inteligenta.

26 - 3

He works out every day.
Li ekzercas ĉiutage.

26 - 4

I can't get out.
Mi ne povas eliri.

26 - 5

Did our client arrive?
Ĉu nia kliento alvenis?

26 - 6

I got it.
Mi ricevis ĝin.

26 - 7

This meat is not fresh.
Ĉi tiu viando ne estas freŝa.

Day 26

Week 4

27 - 1

Don't move!
Ne moviĝu!

27 - 2

She has a little son.
Ŝi havas fileton.

27 - 3

Please forgive me.
Bonvolu pardoni min.

27 - 4

The cake is too sweet.
La kuko estas tro dolĉa.

27 - 5

I really appreciate it.
Mi vere aprezas ĝin.

27 - 6

The food here is bad.
La manĝaĵo ĉi tie estas malbona.

27 - 7

He tested the software.
Li testis la programaron.

Day 27

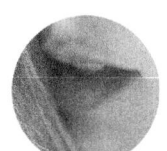

LEARN ESPERANTO IN 52 WEEKS

LEARN ESPERANTO IN 52 WEEKS WITH 7 SENTENCES A DAY

Test 4

28 - 1

The water is soft.

4/52

28 - 2

Did i ask them to wait?

28 - 3

It's too short for me.

28 - 4

Please come at once.

28 - 5

He is smart.

28 - 6

Don't move!

28 - 7

He tested the software.

Day 28

Week 5

29 - 1

Here's my id.
Jen mia identigilo.

29 - 2

Let's try harder.
Ni penu pli forte.

29 - 3

How is everyone?
Kiel ĉiuj fartas?

29 - 4

I'm not sure about it.
Mi ne certas pri tio.

29 - 5

Are you free next week?
Ĉu vi liberas venontsemajne?

29 - 6

Look before you leap.
Rigardu antaŭ ol vi saltas.

29 - 7

How is your mother?
Kiel fartas via patrino?

Day 29

Week 5

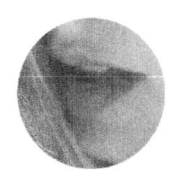

30 - 1

I feel dizzy.
Mi sentas kapturnon.

30 - 2

Who else wants to try?
Kiu alia volas provi?

30 - 3

See you later.
Ĝis revido.

30 - 4

Please hurry!
Bonvolu rapidi!

30 - 5

He led her in the dance.
Li gvidis ŝin en la danco.

30 - 6

It's very cheap.
Ĝi estas tre malmultekosta.

30 - 7

What turns you on?
Kio ŝaltas vin?

Day 30

Week 5

31 - 1
A stick of butter.
Bastono da butero.

31 - 2
He is on the other line.
Li estas sur la alia linio.

31 - 3
Let's go home together.
Ni kune iru hejmen.

31 - 4
I don't agree.
Mi ne konsentas.

31 - 5
I am friendly.
Mi estas amika.

31 - 6
I am on a diet.
Mi estas dieto.

31 - 7
My father snores loudly.
Mia patro laŭte ronkas.

Day 31

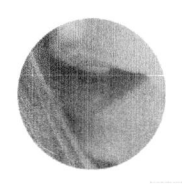

Week 5

32 - 1

Who is not here today?
Kiu ne estas ĉi tie hodiaŭ?

32 - 2

He's a rational person.
Li estas racia homo.

32 - 3

There's no other way.
Ne estas alia maniero.

32 - 4

Motivate yourself.
Motivigu vin.

32 - 5

Hi! how are you doing?
Saluton! kiel vi fartas?

32 - 6

She loves festivals.
Ŝi amas festivalojn.

32 - 7

I can't breathe.
Mi ne povas spiri.

Day 32

Week 5

33 - 1

Please check the oil.
Bonvolu kontroli la oleon.

33 - 2

That movie was boring.
Tiu filmo estis enuiga.

33 - 3

Merry christmas!.
Feliĉan kristnaskon!.

33 - 4

I need home insurance.
Mi bezonas hejman asekuron.

33 - 5

It's too expensive.
Ĝi estas tro multekosta.

33 - 6

She has big legs.
Ŝi havas grandajn krurojn.

33 - 7

He is very hadworking.
Li estas tre laborema.

Day 33

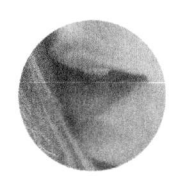

Week 5

34 - 1

Please try this dish.
Bonvolu provi ĉi tiun pladon.

34 - 2

She loves to dance.
Ŝi amas danci.

34 - 3

I belong to new york.
Mi apartenas al novjorko.

34 - 4

Don't you have change?
Ĉu vi ne havas ŝanĝon?

34 - 5

Have a nice day!
Havu bonan tagon!

34 - 6

Let's go home.
Ni iru hejmen.

34 - 7

Just take it easy.
Simple prenu ĝin trankvila.

Day 34

Test 5

35 - 1

Look before you leap.

35 - 2

He led her in the dance.

35 - 3

I don't agree.

35 - 4

There's no other way.

35 - 5

That movie was boring.

35 - 6

Please try this dish.

35 - 7

Just take it easy.

Day 35

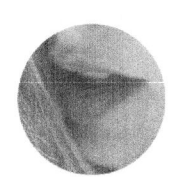

Week 6

36 - 1
My mother sighed.
Mia patrino suspiris.

36 - 2
Don't make me angry.
Ne koleru min.

36 - 3
She is cold.
Ŝi estas malvarma.

36 - 4
I'll put you through.
Mi trapasos vin.

36 - 5
He is motivated to work.
Li estas motivita labori.

36 - 6
She likes traveling.
Ŝi ŝatas vojaĝi.

36 - 7
Your tickets, please.
Viajn biletojn, mi petas.

Day 36

Week 6

37 - 1

Keep the change.
Konservi la ŝanĝon.

37 - 2

These grapes are sour.
Ĉi tiuj vinberoj estas acidaj.

37 - 3

She sued the company.
Ŝi jurpersekutis la firmaon.

37 - 4

Did he come?
Ĉu li venis?

37 - 5

I owe you a great deal.
Mi multe ŝuldas al vi.

37 - 6

Please do not litter.
Bonvolu ne rubujo.

37 - 7

My friend is over there.
Mia amiko estas tie.

Day 37

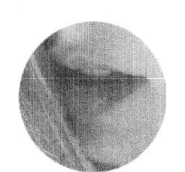

Week 6

38 - 1

Have you been abroad?
Ĉu vi estis eksterlande?

38 - 2

Are you awake?
Ĉu vi vekas?

38 - 3

A roll of tissue.
Rulo de histo.

38 - 4

Sorry about that.
Pardonon pri tio.

38 - 5

Solve it on the board.
Solvu ĝin sur la tabulo.

38 - 6

I loathe ironing.
Mi abomenas gladi.

38 - 7

How is he doing?
Kiel li fartas?

Day 38

Week 6

39 - 1

We have plenty of time.
Ni havas multe da tempo.

39 - 2

Where are you working?
Kie vi laboras?

39 - 3

He is badly injured.
Li estas grave vundita.

39 - 4

I like old cars.
Mi ŝatas malnovajn aŭtojn.

39 - 5

Any message please?
Iu mesaĝo bonvolu?

39 - 6

Don't shout.
Ne kriu.

39 - 7

It was a touching film.
Ĝi estis kortuŝa filmo.

Day 39

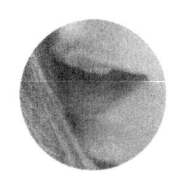

Week 6

40 - 1

I've been attacked.
Mi estis atakita.

40 - 2

You are so kind.
Vi estas tiel afabla.

40 - 3

What time does it end?
Je kioma horo ĝi finiĝas?

40 - 4

How do i go about?
Kiel mi faru?

40 - 5

I am doing business.
Mi faras komercon.

40 - 6

Don't mention it.
Ne menciu ĝin.

40 - 7

Always wash your hands.
Ĉiam lavu viajn manojn.

Day 40

Week 6

41 - 1

Do you know that girl?
Ĉu vi konas tiun knabinon?

41 - 2

Sorry i am late.
Pardonu, mi malfruas.

41 - 3

That's a great idea.
Tio estas bonega ideo.

41 - 4

Please stand up.
Bonvolu ekstari.

41 - 5

I got a new job.
Mi ricevis novan laboron.

41 - 6

Listen to me.
Aŭskultu min.

41 - 7

Did i ask you?
Ĉu mi demandis vin?

Day 41

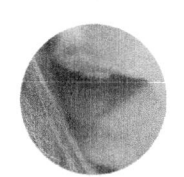

Test 6

42 - 1

She likes traveling.

42 - 2

I owe you a great deal.

42 - 3

Sorry about that.

42 - 4

He is badly injured.

42 - 5

You are so kind.

42 - 6

Do you know that girl?

42 - 7

Did i ask you?

Day 42

Week 7

43 - 1
Hi jack. i'm sophia.
Saluton jack. mi estas sofia.

43 - 2
Yes. i have.
Jes. mi havas.

43 - 3
Why is he dull?
Kial li estas obtuza?

43 - 4
This is for you.
Tio estas por vi.

43 - 5
That's very kind of you.
Tio estas tre afabla de vi.

43 - 6
He's a famous singer.
Li estas fama kantisto.

43 - 7
I'm off work tomorrow.
Mi estas de laboro morgaŭ.

Day 43

Week 7

44 - 1
Does the boy arise?
Ĉu la knabo leviĝas?

44 - 2
I keep my books here.
Mi konservas miajn librojn ĉi tie.

44 - 3
It is already 8.30.
Jam estas la 8.30.

44 - 4
He's a cunning man.
Li estas ruza viro.

44 - 5
Sorry, it's my fault.
Pardonu, estas mia kulpo.

44 - 6
I'm lost.
Mi estas perdita.

44 - 7
I'm sleepy.
Mi estas dormema.

Day 44

Week 7

45 - 1

I like bitter coffee.
Mi ŝatas amaran kafon.

45 - 2

I had cake for dessert.
Mi havis kukon por deserto.

45 - 3

I like a darker one.
Mi ŝatas pli malhelan.

45 - 4

Can i try it on, please?
Ĉu mi povas provi ĝin, mi petas?

45 - 5

Can i pay by cheque?
Ĉu mi povas pagi per ĉeko?

45 - 6

My shoes got dirty.
Miaj ŝuoj malpuriĝis.

45 - 7

All the best.
Ĉion bonan.

Day 45

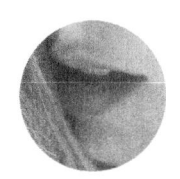

Week 7

46 - 1

Where did you meet him?
Kie vi renkontis lin?

46 - 2

Whose parcel is this?
Kies pakaĵo estas ĉi tiu?

46 - 3

See you next time.
Vidi vin venontfoje.

46 - 4

This road is bumpy.
Ĉi tiu vojo estas malebena.

46 - 5

It's very cool today.
Estas tre mojose hodiaŭ.

46 - 6

No, that's not true.
Ne, tio ne estas vera.

46 - 7

She said so.
Ŝi diris tiel.

Day 46

Week 7

47 - 1

I feel very tired.
Mi sentas min tre laca.

47 - 2

Where is the exit?
Kie estas la elirejo?

47 - 3

She's wearing boots.
Ŝi portas botojn.

47 - 4

Your pulse is weak.
Via pulso estas malforta.

47 - 5

He came to my office.
Li venis al mia oficejo.

47 - 6

My father's a lawyer.
Mia patro estas advokato.

47 - 7

I have office tomorrow.
Mi havas oficejon morgaŭ.

Day 47

Week 7

48 - 1

I have a big dream.
Mi havas grandan sonĝon.

48 - 2

A fly is buzzing.
Muŝo zumas.

48 - 3

I am nervous.
Mi estas nervoza.

48 - 4

I heard a gunshot.
Mi aŭdis pafon.

48 - 5

He fired the servant.
Li maldungis la serviston.

48 - 6

Please pass me the salt.
Bonvolu pasi al mi la salon.

48 - 7

Did he attempt?
Ĉu li provis?

Day 48

Test 7

49 - 1

He's a famous singer.

49 - 2

Sorry, it's my fault.

49 - 3

Can i try it on, please?

49 - 4

See you next time.

49 - 5

Where is the exit?

49 - 6

I have a big dream.

49 - 7

Did he attempt?

Day 49

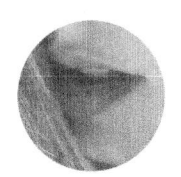

Week 8

50 - 1

I need more exercise.
Mi bezonas pli da ekzercado.

50 - 2

I told him everything.
Mi ĉion rakontis al li.

50 - 3

It is such a lovely day.
Estas tiel bela tago.

50 - 4

Reduce the volume.
Redukti la volumon.

50 - 5

They live a quiet life.
Ili vivas trankvilan vivon.

50 - 6

This is a lonely song.
Ĉi tio estas soleca kanto.

50 - 7

Is this reduced?
Ĉu ĉi tio estas reduktita?

Day 50

Week 8

51 - 1
My friend defended me.
Mia amiko defendis min.

51 - 2
He came here.
Li venis ĉi tien.

51 - 3
How was your flight?
Kiel estis via flugo?

51 - 4
No entry for buses.
Neniu eniro por busoj.

51 - 5
I have no problem.
Mi ne havas problemon.

51 - 6
That's awful.
Tio estas terura.

51 - 7
My father yawned.
Mia patro oscedis.

Day 51

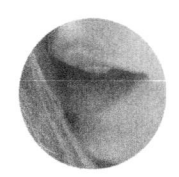

Week 8

52 - 1

It wasn't me.
Ne estis mi.

52 - 2

Has anyone seen my bag?
Ĉu iu vidis mian sakon?

52 - 3

I'm good at science.
Mi estas bona pri scienco.

52 - 4

Let's keep in touch!
Ni konservu kontakton!

52 - 5

That's so kind of you.
Tio estas tiel afabla de vi.

52 - 6

Thank you.
Dankon.

52 - 7

How is your sister?
Kiel fartas via fratino?

Day 52

Week 8

53 - 1

I drank a little wine.
Mi trinkis iom da vino.

53 - 2

In what price range?
En kiu prezo gamo?

53 - 3

Any ideas?
Ĉu iuj ideoj?

53 - 4

Did you lock the door?
Ĉu vi ŝlosis la pordon?

53 - 5

Do you have any doubt?
Ĉu vi havas ian dubon?

53 - 6

It's been a while.
Jam pasis kelka tempo.

53 - 7

We had a smooth landing.
Ni havis glatan surteriĝon.

Day 53

Week 8

54 - 1

Don't skip meals.
Ne saltu manĝojn.

54 - 2

Her fingers are thin.
Ŝiaj fingroj estas maldikaj.

54 - 3

My son is left-handed.
Mia filo estas maldekstramana.

54 - 4

Raise your pencils.
Levu viajn krajonojn.

54 - 5

The engine won't start.
La motoro ne startos.

54 - 6

I have got a puncture.
Mi havas trapikon.

54 - 7

I have a stomachache.
Mi havas stomakdoloron.

Day 54

Week 8

55 - 1
I can't read a map.
Mi ne povas legi mapon.

55 - 2
Shall i make tea?
Ĉu mi faru teon?

55 - 3
I have a backache.
Mi havas dorsdoloron.

55 - 4
Thunder is rumbling.
Tondro bruas.

55 - 5
We took a package tour.
Ni faris pakvojaĝon.

55 - 6
This chair is shaky.
Ĉi tiu seĝo tremas.

55 - 7
Why did you call him?
Kial vi vokis lin?

Day 55

Test 8

56 - 1

This is a lonely song.

56 - 2

I have no problem.

8/52

56 - 3

Let's keep in touch!

56 - 4

Any ideas?

56 - 5

Her fingers are thin.

56 - 6

I can't read a map.

56 - 7

Why did you call him?

Day 56

Week 9

9/52

57 - 1

I'll pay for that.
Mi pagos por tio.

57 - 2

I am very strict.
Mi estas tre strikta.

57 - 3

She left a message.
Ŝi lasis mesaĝon.

57 - 4

Bye. take care.
Adiaŭ. zorgu.

57 - 5

I bought three glasses.
Mi aĉetis tri glasojn.

57 - 6

I understand.
Mi komprenas.

57 - 7

He scored three goals.
Li trafis tri golojn.

Day 57

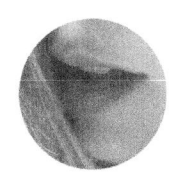

Week 9

58 - 1

That is common sense.
Tio estas komuna racio.

58 - 2

I'm from the u.s.
Mi estas el usono

58 - 3

I'm truly sorry.
Mi vere bedaŭras.

58 - 4

It's your fault.
Estas via kulpo.

58 - 5

I had twin baby girls.
Mi havis ĝemelajn knabinetojn.

58 - 6

Can you play the piano?
Ĉu vi povas ludi pianon?

58 - 7

He is my husband.
Li estas mia edzo.

Day 58

Week 9

59 - 1

I'm unemployed.
Mi estas senlabora.

59 - 2

Take them with you.
Prenu ilin kun vi.

59 - 3

It's a waste of time.
Estas tempoperdo.

59 - 4

Next please.
Poste mi petas.

59 - 5

No, thanks.
Ne, dankon.

59 - 6

What time do you open?
Je kioma horo vi malfermas?

59 - 7

Any questions?
Ĉu demandoj?

Day 59

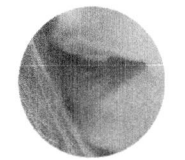

Week 9

60 - 1

Her hair is very long.
Ŝia hararo estas tre longa.

60 - 2

Will you marry me?
Ĉu vi edzigos min?

60 - 3

I had cookies and tea.
Mi havis kuketojn kaj teon.

60 - 4

Ok, i'll take this one.
Bone, mi prenos ĉi tiun.

60 - 5

How did he come?
Kiel li venis?

60 - 6

It's monday again.
Denove estas lundo.

60 - 7

It's too tight.
Ĝi estas tro streĉa.

Day 60

Week 9

61 - 1

She writes left-handed.
Ŝi skribas maldekstramane.

61 - 2

How do i know that?
Kiel mi scias tion?

61 - 3

It's not true.
Tio ne estas vera.

61 - 4

You don't have to wait.
Vi ne devas atendi.

61 - 5

A full glass of milk.
Plena glaso da lakto.

61 - 6

He clenched his fists.
Li kunpremis la pugnojn.

61 - 7

Sea water is salty.
Mara akvo estas sala.

Day 61

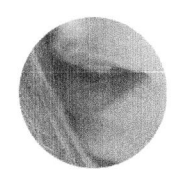

Week 9

62 - 1

It's not a big deal.
Ne estas granda afero.

62 - 2

I want to go shopping!
Mi volas butikumi!

62 - 3

He is my neighbour.
Li estas mia najbaro.

62 - 4

Is the story real?
Ĉu la rakonto estas vera?

62 - 5

She was very pleased.
Ŝi estis tre kontenta.

62 - 6

Just stay focused.
Nur restu koncentrita.

62 - 7

He is not a bad person.
Li ne estas malbona homo.

Day 62

Test 9

63 - 1

I understand.

63 - 2

I had twin baby girls.

63 - 3

Next please.

63 - 4

I had cookies and tea.

63 - 5

How do i know that?

63 - 6

It's not a big deal.

63 - 7

He is not a bad person.

Day 63

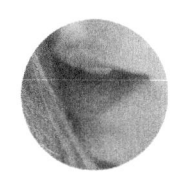

Week 10

64 - 1

He threw the ball.
Li ĵetis la pilkon.

64 - 2

I don't understand why.
Mi ne komprenas kial.

64 - 3

Call an ambulance.
Voku ambulancon.

64 - 4

The ship is sinking.
La ŝipo sinkas.

64 - 5

Here is your tip.
Jen via konsileto.

64 - 6

We drink tea every day.
Ni trinkas teon ĉiutage.

64 - 7

Speak louder, please.
Parolu pli laŭte, mi petas.

Day 64

Week 10

65 - 1
May i come in?
Ĉu mi rajtas enveni?

65 - 2
You are beautiful.
Vi estas bela.

65 - 3
Can anyone hear me?
Ĉu iu povas aŭdi min?

65 - 4
Does the dog bite?
Ĉu la hundo mordas?

65 - 5
How is the new house?
Kiel fartas la nova domo?

65 - 6
Are you in the queue?
Ĉu vi estas en la vico?

65 - 7
I have a car.
Mi havas aŭton.

Day 65

Week 10

66 - 1

When is he expected?
Kiam oni atendas lin?

66 - 2

Are you ready?
Ĉu vi pretas?

66 - 3

Who do you live with?
Kun kiu vi loĝas?

66 - 4

Do you have a match?
Ĉu vi havas matĉon?

66 - 5

Get out of here!
Foriru de ĉi tie!

66 - 6

I feel tired.
Mi sentas min laca.

66 - 7

He burned his hand.
Li bruligis sian manon.

Day 66

Week 10

67 - 1

I do not feel well.
Mi ne sentas min bone.

67 - 2

That would be okay.
Tio estus bone.

67 - 3

It is very hot inside.
Estas tre varme interne.

67 - 4

What date is today?
Kio dato estas hodiaŭ?

67 - 5

I'm physically strong.
Mi estas fizike forta.

67 - 6

How old are you?
Kiom da jaroj vi havas?

67 - 7

Give it to them.
Donu ĝin al ili.

Day 67

Week 10

68 - 1

I have a dull feeling.
Mi havas obtuzan senton.

68 - 2

Your sister is kind.
Via fratino estas afabla.

68 - 3

It's ten o'clock.
Estas la deka.

68 - 4

I completely agree.
Mi tute konsentas.

68 - 5

It's clearly his fault.
Estas klare lia kulpo.

68 - 6

It is forbidden to.
Estas malpermesite.

68 - 7

Are your equipment new?
Ĉu via ekipaĵo estas nova?

Day 68

Week 10

69 - 1
My car is broken.
Mia aŭto estas rompita.

69 - 2
Do not disturb.
Ne ĝenu.

69 - 3
Could i use your phone?
Ĉu mi povus uzi vian telefonon?

69 - 4
He's wearing glasses.
Li portas okulvitrojn.

69 - 5
Please don't be so sad.
Bonvolu ne esti tiel malĝoja.

69 - 6
He owns three cars.
Li posedas tri aŭtojn.

69 - 7
Bless you!
Sanon!

Day 69

Test 10

70 - 1

We drink tea every day.

70 - 2

How is the new house?

70 - 3

Do you have a match?

70 - 4

It is very hot inside.

70 - 5

Your sister is kind.

70 - 6

My car is broken.

70 - 7

Bless you!

Day 70

LEARN ESPERANTO IN 52 WEEKS

LEARN ESPERANTO IN 52 WEEKS WITH 7 SENTENCES A DAY

Week 11

71 - 1

No passing.
Neniu preterpaso.

71 - 2

He's a nasty man.
Li estas malbona viro.

11/52

71 - 3

How many people?
Kiom da homoj?

71 - 4

Where's the florist's?
Kie estas la floristo?

71 - 5

A handful of beans.
Manpleno da faboj.

71 - 6

I just love summer.
Mi nur amas someron.

71 - 7

That sounds nice.
Tio sonas bele.

Day 71

Week 11

72 - 1

What is your occupation?
Kio estas via okupo?

72 - 2

Stop talking, please.
Ĉesu paroli, mi petas.

72 - 3

That's not always true.
Tio ne ĉiam veras.

72 - 4

I go to school by train.
Mi iras al lernejo per trajno.

72 - 5

She was operated on.
Ŝi estis operaciita.

72 - 6

Hang on for a moment.
Atendu por momento.

72 - 7

It is straight ahead.
Ĝi estas rekte antaŭen.

Day 72

Week 11

73 - 1

Don't get angry.
Ne koleru.

73 - 2

He took off his glasses.
Li demetis siajn okulvitrojn.

73 - 3

Good night.
Bonan nokton.

73 - 4

Do you work on sundays?
Ĉu vi laboras dimanĉe?

73 - 5

The snow has piled up.
La neĝo amasiĝis.

73 - 6

Where have you been?
Kie vi estis?

73 - 7

Let's take a break.
Ni faru paŭzon.

Day 73

Week 11

74 - 1
I ate a slice of cheese.
Mi manĝis trancajon da fromaĝo.

74 - 2
What do you mean?
Kion vi celas?

74 - 3
Where is the post box?
Kie estas la poŝtkesto?

74 - 4
This is very important.
Ĉi tio estas tre grava.

74 - 5
What a cheeky fellow!
Kia impertinenta ulo!

74 - 6
I didn't know that song.
Mi ne konis tiun kanton.

74 - 7
I handed him the letter.
Mi transdonis al li la leteron.

Day 74

Week 11

75 - 1

What time is it leaving?
Je kioma horo ĝi foriras?

75 - 2

He is fine.
Li fartas bone.

75 - 3

Sunglasses suit him.
Sunokulvitroj konvenas al li.

75 - 4

That was excellent.
Tio estis bonega.

75 - 5

So what?
Do kio?

75 - 6

She reacted well.
Ŝi bone reagis.

75 - 7

Do you serve alcohol?
Ĉu vi servas alkoholon?

Day 75

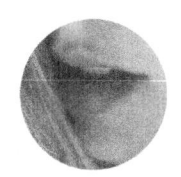

Week 11

76 - 1

I like reading books.
Mi ŝatas legi librojn.

76 - 2

What a nice apartment.
Kia bela apartamento.

11/52

76 - 3

I totally disagree.
Mi tute malkonsentas.

76 - 4

He is a radiographer.
Li estas radiografo.

76 - 5

Her skin is smooth.
Ŝia haŭto estas glata.

76 - 6

It was my pleasure.
Estis mia plezuro.

76 - 7

No, i don't mind.
Ne, mi ne ĝenas.

Day 76

Test 11

77 - 1

I just love summer.

77 - 2

She was operated on.

77 - 3

Do you work on sundays?

77 - 4

Where is the post box?

77 - 5

He is fine.

77 - 6

I like reading books.

77 - 7

No, i don't mind.

Day 77

Week 12

78 - 1

This door is automatic.
Ĉi tiu pordo estas aŭtomata.

78 - 2

I know how it feels.
Mi scias kiel ĝi sentas.

78 - 3

This meat is greasy.
Ĉi tiu viando estas grasa.

78 - 4

He is very smart.
Li estas tre saĝa.

78 - 5

I will not buy it.
Mi ne aĉetos ĝin.

78 - 6

Trust me, i can do it.
Fidu min, mi povas fari ĝin.

78 - 7

How tall are you?
Kiom alta vi estas?

Day 78

Week 12

79 - 1
I have an idea.
Mi havas ideo.

79 - 2
My father loves fishing.
Mia patro amas fiŝkapti.

79 - 3
Please keep working.
Bonvolu daŭrigi labori.

79 - 4
Yes, i'd love too.
Jes, ankaŭ mi amus.

79 - 5
I work as a professor.
Mi laboras kiel profesoro.

79 - 6
My room is small.
Mia ĉambro estas malgranda.

79 - 7
Who's calling, please?
Kiu vokas, mi petas?

Day 79

Week 12

80 - 1
I don't mind.
Mi ne ĝenas.

80 - 2
Someone stole my bag.
Iu ŝtelis mian sakon.

80 - 3
He owes me one.
Li ŝuldas al mi unu.

80 - 4
Give me a life vest.
Donu al mi savveston.

80 - 5
How is it?
Kiel ĝi estas?

80 - 6
How have you been?
Kiel vi estis fartanta?

80 - 7
Describe yourself.
Priskribu vin.

Day 80

Week 12

81 - 1
I bought a red rose.
Mi aĉetis ruĝan rozon.

81 - 2
Calm down.
Trankviliĝu.

81 - 3
This dish is tasteless.
Ĉi tiu plado estas sengusta.

81 - 4
First aid center.
Centro de unua helpo.

81 - 5
I'm against it.
Mi estas kontraŭ ĝi.

81 - 6
No, i'm serious.
Ne, mi estas serioza.

81 - 7
He loaded the pistol.
Li ŝargis la pistolon.

Day 81

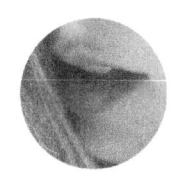

Week 12

82 - 1

She is my mother.
Ŝi estas mia patrino.

82 - 2

It's my duty to do it.
Estas mia devo fari ĝin.

82 - 3

Her face is pale.
Ŝia vizaĝo estas pala.

82 - 4

He used to be poor.
Li antaŭe estis malriĉa.

82 - 5

I need to earn money.
Mi bezonas gajni monon.

82 - 6

I marked the mistakes.
Mi markis la erarojn.

82 - 7

He is a fine poet.
Li estas bonega poeto.

Day 82

Week 12

83 - 1

Dry in the shade.
Sekigi en la ombro.

83 - 2

I'm glad to see you.
Mi ĝojas vidi vin.

83 - 3

I got up at seven today.
Mi ellitiĝis hodiaŭ je la sepa.

83 - 4

Show me our sales.
Montru al mi niajn vendojn.

83 - 5

I found a new job.
Mi trovis novan laboron.

83 - 6

I work from home.
Mi laboras de hejmo.

83 - 7

Who is he?
Kiu li estas?

Day 83

LEARN ESPERANTO IN 52 WEEKS

LEARN ESPERANTO IN 52 WEEKS WITH 7 SENTENCES A DAY

Test 12

84 - 1

Trust me, i can do it.

84 - 2

I work as a professor.

12/52

84 - 3

Give me a life vest.

84 - 4

This dish is tasteless.

84 - 5

It's my duty to do it.

84 - 6

Dry in the shade.

84 - 7

Who is he?

Day 84

Week 13

85 - 1
I got an email from him.
Mi ricevis retmesaĝon de li.

85 - 2
That child is so thin.
Tiu infano estas tiel maldika.

85 - 3
Sure, go ahead.
Certe, iru antaŭen.

85 - 4
I am happy today.
Mi estas feliĉa hodiaŭ.

85 - 5
He has no time.
Li ne havas tempon.

85 - 6
He's acting strange.
Li agas strange.

85 - 7
What will you do?
Kion vi faros?

Day 85

Week 13

86 - 1

Very good!
Tre bona!

86 - 2

I have no objection.
Mi ne havas objêton.

86 - 3

Is this on sale?
Ĉu ĉi tio estas vendata?

86 - 4

Your bag is light.
Via sako estas malpeza.

86 - 5

A sprig of parsley.
Rameto da petroselo.

86 - 6

No, i'd rather not.
Ne, mi preferas ne.

86 - 7

Does he befit always?
Ĉu li ĉiam konvenas?

Day 86

Week 13

87 - 1
He no longer hates her.
Li ne plu malamas ŝin.

87 - 2
Don't you have a pen?
Ĉu vi ne havas plumon?

87 - 3
He is hungry.
Li estas malsata.

87 - 4
She shed tears.
Ŝi verŝis larmojn.

87 - 5
He came here yesterday.
Li venis ĉi tien hieraŭ.

87 - 6
I sealed the letter.
Mi sigelis la leteron.

87 - 7
Shall we start?
Ĉu ni komencu?

Day 87

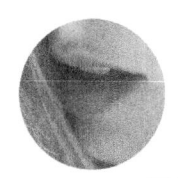

Week 13

88 - 1

Mind your business.
Atentu viajn aferojn.

88 - 2

Emergency telephone.
Urĝa telefono.

88 - 3

Add a little more salt.
Aldonu iom pli da salo.

88 - 4

He is ten years old.
Li estas dekjara.

88 - 5

The server is down.
La servilo malfunkcias.

88 - 6

Did she ask me?
Ĉu ŝi demandis min?

88 - 7

Forget the past.
Forgesu la pasintecon.

Day 88

Week 13

89 - 1

See you.
Ĝis revido.

89 - 2

He's good at singing.
Li lertas pri kantado.

89 - 3

Be careful.
Atentu.

89 - 4

He could not come today.
Li ne povis veni hodiaŭ.

89 - 5

This seat is taken.
Ĉi tiu sidloko estas prenita.

89 - 6

Have a nice weekend.
Bonan semajnfinon.

89 - 7

When can i talk to you?
Kiam mi povas paroli kun vi?

Day 89

Week 13

90 - 1

He majors in physics.
Li specialiĝas pri fiziko.

90 - 2

My boss is very strict.
Mia estro estas tre strikta.

90 - 3

Let me check for you.
Lasu min kontroli por vi.

90 - 4

I don't have time.
Mi ne havas tempon.

90 - 5

Thanks, i'll do it.
Dankon, mi faros ĝin.

90 - 6

Please boil some water.
Bonvolu boli iom da akvo.

90 - 7

He's older than me.
Li estas pli maljuna ol mi.

Day 90

Test 13

91 - 1

He's acting strange.

91 - 2

A sprig of parsley.

91 - 3

She shed tears.

91 - 4

Add a little more salt.

91 - 5

He's good at singing.

91 - 6

He majors in physics.

91 - 7

He's older than me.

Day 91

LEARN ESPERANTO IN 52 WEEKS
LEARN ESPERANTO IN 52 WEEKS WITH 7 SENTENCES A DAY

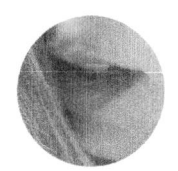

Week 14

92 - 1

What's your surname?
Kio estas via familia nomo?

92 - 2

It does not fit my size.
Ĝi ne konvenas al mia grandeco.

92 - 3

A bird is flying.
Birdo flugas.

92 - 4

Does the dog bark?
Ĉu la hundo bojas?

92 - 5

How do you do?
Kiel vi fartas?

92 - 6

Today is my birthday.
Hodiaŭ estas mia naskiĝtago.

92 - 7

I sorted out my clothes.
Mi ordigis miajn vestaĵojn.

Day 92

Week 14

93 - 1

I'll pay in cash.
Mi pagos kontante.

93 - 2

How long will it take?
Kiom da tempo ĝi daŭros?

93 - 3

What a letdown.
Kia laso.

93 - 4

I'm going to undress.
Mi tuj senvestiĝos.

93 - 5

Could i have a refund?
Ĉu mi povus havi repagon?

93 - 6

He speaks clearly.
Li parolas klare.

93 - 7

My wallet was stolen.
Mia monujo estis ŝtelita.

Day 93

Week 14

94 - 1

Please help me out sir.
Bonvolu helpi min, sinjoro.

94 - 2

It's half past eleven.
Estas duono post la dekunua.

94 - 3

No, thank you.
Ne dankon.

94 - 4

Next, you.
Poste, vi.

94 - 5

What day is today?
Kiu tago estas hodiaŭ?

94 - 6

He likes spicy food.
Li ŝatas spican manĝaĵon.

94 - 7

Let it go.
Lasu ĝin iri.

Day 94

Week 14

95 - 1

You've made my day.
Vi faris mian tagon.

95 - 2

He's greedy for money.
Li estas avida je mono.

95 - 3

Hazardous waste.
Danĝera rubo.

95 - 4

He hates evil.
Li malamas malbonon.

95 - 5

I am a vegetarian.
Mi estas vegetarano.

95 - 6

I am terribly sorry.
Mi terure bedaŭras.

95 - 7

Absolutely not.
Absolute ne.

Day 95

LEARN ESPERANTO IN 52 WEEKS WITH 7 SENTENCES A DAY

Week 14

96 - 1
It's a kind of fruit.
Ĝi estas speco de frukto.

96 - 2
Our cat is a male.
Nia kato estas masklo.

96 - 3
Goodbye.
Adiaŭ.

96 - 4
Is the machine working?
Ĉu la maŝino funkcias?

96 - 5
Thanks a lot.
Multaj dankoj.

96 - 6
Please imitate my move.
Bonvolu imiti mian movon.

96 - 7
Let's share duties.
Ni dividu devojn.

Day 96

Week 14

97 - 1

How big is that house?
Kiom granda estas tiu domo?

97 - 2

What a stubborn child!
Kia obstina infano!

97 - 3

Don't tell lies.
Ne diru mensogojn.

97 - 4

Is it true?
Ĉu vere?

97 - 5

Complete the table.
Kompletigu la tabelon.

97 - 6

Perfect!
Perfekta!

97 - 7

How is this cooked?
Kiel ĉi tio estas kuirita?

Day 97

LEARN ESPERANTO IN 52 WEEKS

LEARN ESPERANTO IN 52 WEEKS WITH 7 SENTENCES A DAY

Test 14

98 - 1

Today is my birthday.

98 - 2

Could i have a refund?

98 - 3

Next, you.

98 - 4

Hazardous waste.

98 - 5

Our cat is a male.

98 - 6

How big is that house?

98 - 7

How is this cooked?

Day 98

Week 15

99 - 1

Do not wet clean.
Ne malseke purigu.

99 - 2

Would you mind?
Ĉu vi bonvolus?

15/52

99 - 3

This cat is a female.
Ĉi tiu kato estas ino.

99 - 4

Oh, that's terrible.
Ho, tio estas terura.

99 - 5

Bring them here.
Alportu ilin ĉi tien.

99 - 6

He got the silver medal.
Li ricevis la arĝentan medalon.

99 - 7

She's with me.
Ŝi estas kun mi.

Day 99

LEARN ESPERANTO IN 52 WEEKS
LEARN ESPERANTO IN 52 WEEKS WITH 7 SENTENCES A DAY

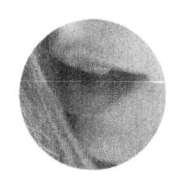

Week 15

100 - 1

I have a fever.
Mi havas febron.

100 - 2

The knife cuts well.
La tranĉilo tranĉas bone.

100 - 3

I decided to marry her.
Mi decidis edziĝi kun ŝi.

100 - 4

He is a national hero.
Li estas nacia heroo.

100 - 5

A spoonful of honey.
Kulero da mielo.

100 - 6

My luggage is lost.
Mia pakaĵo estas perdita.

100 - 7

It's sorching hoait.
Estas sorĉa hoait.

Day 100

LEARN ESPERANTO IN 52 WEEKS

LEARN ESPERANTO IN 52 WEEKS WITH 7 SENTENCES A DAY

Week 15

101 - 1

This pencil is sharp.
Ĉi tiu krajono estas akra.

101 - 2

You can't.
Vi ne povas.

15/52

101 - 3

He's a great scholar.
Li estas bonega akademiulo.

101 - 4

I am bold.
Mi estas aŭdaca.

101 - 5

Wake him up.
Veku lin.

101 - 6

I've fully recovered.
Mi plene resaniĝis.

101 - 7

I need health insurance.
Mi bezonas sanasekuron.

Day 101

LEARN ESPERANTO IN 52 WEEKS

LEARN ESPERANTO IN 52 WEEKS WITH 7 SENTENCES A DAY

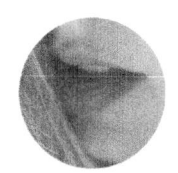

Week 15

102 - 1

Follow the signs.
Sekvu la signojn.

102 - 2

Don't talk to me.
Ne parolu al mi.

102 - 3

The bath is ready.
La bano estas preta.

102 - 4

He has office today.
Li havas oficejon hodiaŭ.

102 - 5

How late is it?
Kiom malfrue estas?

102 - 6

I feel feverish.
Mi sentas febron.

102 - 7

When is she coming?
Kiam ŝi venos?

Day 102

Week 15

103 - 1

It's very nice of you.
Estas tre afabla de vi.

103 - 2

Good job.
Bona laboro.

103 - 3

He is unconscious.
Li estas senkonscia.

103 - 4

Did anybody come?
Ĉu iu venis?

103 - 5

No, i did not do it.
Ne, mi ne faris ĝin.

103 - 6

How about three o'clock?
Kiom pri la tria horo?

103 - 7

I don't have time now.
Mi ne havas tempon nun.

Day 103

Week 15

104 - 1

This match is a draw.
Ĉi tiu matĉo estas remizo.

104 - 2

The bath was lukewarm.
La bano estis varmeta.

104 - 3

He loves himself.
Li amas sin mem.

104 - 4

I am terrified.
Mi estas terurita.

104 - 5

Alcohol is colorless.
Alkoholo estas senkolora.

104 - 6

Swallows are flying.
Hirundoj flugas.

104 - 7

How is the weather like?
Kiel estas la vetero?

Day 104

Test 15

105 - 1

He got the silver medal.

105 - 2

A spoonful of honey.

105 - 3

I am bold.

105 - 4

The bath is ready.

105 - 5

Good job.

105 - 6

This match is a draw.

105 - 7

How is the weather like?

Day 105

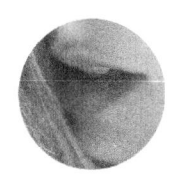

Week 16

106 - 1

Turn around.
Turnu vin.

106 - 2

He broke his promise.
Li rompis sian promeson.

106 - 3

That's all right.
Tio estas bone.

106 - 4

Who cares.
Kiu zorgas.

106 - 5

I can't afford it.
Mi ne povas pagi ĝin.

106 - 6

Congratulations!
Gratulon!

106 - 7

Pork is delicious.
Porkaĵo estas bongusta.

Day 106

Week 16

107 - 1

Thanks for the tip.
Dankon pro la konsileto.

107 - 2

We entered the woods.
Ni eniris la arbaron.

107 - 3

I love stopovers.
Mi amas haltojn.

107 - 4

I'm quite sure about it.
Mi estas tute certa pri tio.

107 - 5

Let me introduce myself.
Lasu min prezenti min.

107 - 6

Yes, please.
Jes bonvolu.

107 - 7

I have a stomach ache.
Mi havas stomakdoloron.

Day 107

Week 16

108 - 1

The house is roomy.
La domo estas ampleksa.

108 - 2

She has two children.
Ŝi havas du infanojn.

108 - 3

The moon is waxing.
La luno kreskas.

108 - 4

Yes, you can.
Jes vi povas.

108 - 5

She has a lot of dolls.
Ŝi havas multajn pupojn.

108 - 6

It's an industrial city.
Ĝi estas industria urbo.

108 - 7

Sure, i'd be glad to.
Certe, mi ĝojus.

Day 108

Week 16

109 - 1

It was a nice evening.
Estis bela vespero.

109 - 2

Where are you from?
De kie vi estas?

109 - 3

The pain is too much.
La doloro estas tro granda.

109 - 4

This is my friend.
Jen mia amiko.

109 - 5

Buy one get one free.
Aĉetu unu ricevu unu senpage.

109 - 6

The dynamite exploded.
La dinamito eksplodis.

109 - 7

He is my grandfather.
Li estas mia avo.

Day 109

Week 16

110 - 1

Don't confuse me.
Ne konfuzu min.

110 - 2

This is my dream job.
Ĉi tio estas mia reva laboro.

110 - 3

His teeth are white.
Liaj dentoj estas blankaj.

110 - 4

What did you say?
Kion vi diris?

110 - 5

The door bell rang.
La porda sonorilo sonoris.

110 - 6

How is the movie?
Kiel fartas la filmo?

110 - 7

What have you decided?
Kion vi decidis?

Day 110

Week 16

111 - 1

I'm sure about it.
Mi estas certa pri tio.

111 - 2

Stop messing around.
Ĉesu fuŝi.

111 - 3

No big deal.
Ne granda afero.

111 - 4

He is driving too fast.
Li veturas tro rapide.

111 - 5

His company relocated.
Lia firmao translokiĝis.

111 - 6

Here is your change.
Jen via ŝanĝo.

111 - 7

Is it useful?
Ĉu ĝi estas utila?

Day 111

Test 16

112 - 1

Congratulations!

112 - 2

Let me introduce myself.

112 - 3

Yes, you can.

112 - 4

The pain is too much.

112 - 5

This is my dream job.

112 - 6

I'm sure about it.

112 - 7

Is it useful?

Day 112

LEARN ESPERANTO IN 52 WEEKS
LEARN ESPERANTO IN 52 WEEKS WITH 7 SENTENCES A DAY

Week 17

113 - 1

I prefer tea to coffee.
Mi preferas teon ol kafon.

113 - 2

I want to disappear now.
Mi volas malaperi nun.

17/52

113 - 3

It looks great!
Ĝi aspektas bonege!

113 - 4

Did he award him?
Ĉu li premiis lin?

113 - 5

We come from paris.
Ni venas el parizo.

113 - 6

Please go in front.
Bonvolu iri antaŭe.

113 - 7

He's quit smoking now.
Li ĉesis fumi nun.

Day 113

Week 17

114 - 1

The meal is ready.
La manĝo estas preta.

114 - 2

That would be fantastic!
Tio estus mirinda!

114 - 3

Can i borrow a pencil?
Ĉu mi povas prunti krajonon?

114 - 4

You're fired.
Vi estas maldungita.

114 - 5

I don't like him.
Mi ne ŝatas lin.

114 - 6

Please don't be late.
Bonvolu ne malfrui.

114 - 7

I excel in this field.
Mi elstaras en ĉi tiu kampo.

Day 114

Week 17

115 - 1

I believe you.
Mi kredas al vi.

115 - 2

It's going to rain.
Pluvos.

115 - 3

What's happening?
Kio okazas?

115 - 4

Are you employed?
Ĉu vi estas dungita?

115 - 5

I ordered a hamburger.
Mi mendis hamburgeron.

115 - 6

She despised him.
Ŝi malestimis lin.

115 - 7

I owe you an apology.
Mi ŝuldas al vi pardonpeton.

Day 115

Week 17

116 - 1

Attend to the phone.
Atentu la telefonon.

116 - 2

Can i try this on?
Ĉu mi povas provi ĉi tion?

116 - 3

Have lunch.
Tagmanĝas.

116 - 4

I like you.
Mi ŝatas vin.

116 - 5

I am looking for a job.
Mi serĉas laboron.

116 - 6

He has a car.
Li havas aŭton.

116 - 7

Do what you like.
Faru kion vi ŝatas.

Day 116

Week 17

117 - 1

I don't know yet.
Mi ankoraŭ ne scias.

117 - 2

There is an explosion.
Estas eksplodo.

117 - 3

She helped a sick dog.
Ŝi helpis malsanan hundon.

117 - 4

The room light is on.
La ĉambra lumo estas ŝaltita.

117 - 5

It's my fault.
Estas mia kulpo.

117 - 6

He has a good heart.
Li havas bonan koron.

117 - 7

Please wear slippers.
Bonvolu porti pantoflojn.

Day 117

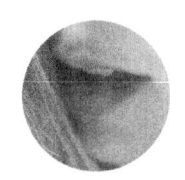

Week 17

118 - 1

Are you ready to order?
Ĉu vi pretas mendi?

118 - 2

I'm lending him a book.
Mi pruntedonas al li libron.

118 - 3

I wrote him a letter.
Mi skribis al li leteron.

17/52

118 - 4

What a nice dress.
Kia bela robo.

118 - 5

He's learning karate.
Li lernas karateon.

118 - 6

He has a weak stomach.
Li havas malfortan stomakon.

118 - 7

I have a scooter.
Mi havas skoteron.

Day 118

LEARN ESPERANTO IN 52 WEEKS

LEARN ESPERANTO IN 52 WEEKS WITH 7 SENTENCES A DAY

Test 17

119 - 1

Please go in front.

119 - 2

I don't like him.

119 - 3

Are you employed?

119 - 4

Have lunch.

119 - 5

There is an explosion.

119 - 6

Are you ready to order?

119 - 7

I have a scooter.

Day 119

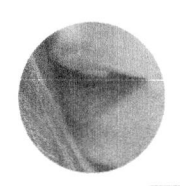

Week 18

120 - 1

What do you do?
Kion vi faras?

120 - 2

Where's the grocer's?
Kie estas la nutraĵvendisto?

120 - 3

Please come here.
Bonvolu veni ĉi tien.

120 - 4

What is his name?
Kio estas lia nomo?

120 - 5

He is my elder brother.
Li estas mia pli aĝa frato.

120 - 6

I like to be alone.
Mi ŝatas esti sola.

120 - 7

Here's thirty dollars.
Jen tridek dolaroj.

Day 120

Week 18

121 - 1

Who called you?
Kiu vokis vin?

121 - 2

He's an actor.
Li estas aktoro.

121 - 3

Long time no see.
Longe ne vidas.

121 - 4

Did you get my letter?
Ĉu vi ricevis mian leteron?

121 - 5

Yes, sir!
Jes sinjoro!

121 - 6

I'll check.
Mi kontrolos.

121 - 7

He's changed a lot.
Li multe ŝanĝiĝis.

Day 121

Week 18

122 - 1

I'm thirsty.
Mi soifas.

122 - 2

I unlaced my shoes.
Mi mallaĉis miajn ŝuojn.

122 - 3

Please open the window.
Bonvolu malfermi la fenestron.

18/52

122 - 4

A pitcher of beer.
Kruĉo da biero.

122 - 5

We are three sisters.
Ni estas tri fratinoj.

122 - 6

Note the address.
Notu la adreson.

122 - 7

The weather is hot.
La vetero estas varma.

Day 122

Week 18

123 - 1
When did you call him?
Kiam vi vokis lin?

123 - 2
Are the shops open?
Ĉu la butikoj estas malfermitaj?

123 - 3
Your table is ready.
Via tablo estas preta.

123 - 4
How long is the film?
Kiom longas la filmo?

123 - 5
Birds flew southward.
Birdoj flugis suden.

123 - 6
I do the paperwork.
Mi faras la paperojn.

123 - 7
Who's next?
Kiu sekvas?

Day 123

Week 18

124 - 1

I sold old books.
Mi vendis malnovajn librojn.

124 - 2

He's good at baseball.
Li lertas pri basbalo.

124 - 3

Call the police.
Voku la policon.

124 - 4

May i borrow your book?
Ĉu mi rajtas prunti vian libron?

124 - 5

I feel hungry.
Mi sentas min malsata.

124 - 6

I don't understand.
Mi ne komprenas.

124 - 7

I forgot my handbag.
Mi forgesis mian mansakon.

Day 124

LEARN ESPERANTO IN 52 WEEKS

LEARN ESPERANTO IN 52 WEEKS WITH 7 SENTENCES A DAY

Week 18

125 - 1

I don't mind it at all.
Mi tute ne ĝenas.

125 - 2

Forget it.
Forgesu ĝin.

125 - 3

Settle down, please.
Restu, mi petas.

18/52

125 - 4

He's a very fun person.
Li estas tre amuza homo.

125 - 5

What is your name?
Kio estas via nomo?

125 - 6

I'm sorry i'm late.
Mi bedaŭras, ke mi malfruas.

125 - 7

The meat is cooked.
La viando estas kuirita.

Day 125

Test 18

126 - 1

I like to be alone.

126 - 2

Yes, sir!

126 - 3

A pitcher of beer.

126 - 4

Your table is ready.

126 - 5

He's good at baseball.

126 - 6

I don't mind it at all.

126 - 7

The meat is cooked.

Day 126

Week 19

127 - 1

When will they come?
Kiam ili venos?

127 - 2

How are things?
Kiel vi fartas?

127 - 3

He executed the plan.
Li efektivigis la planon.

127 - 4

Do not open.
Ne malfermu.

127 - 5

Jokes do have limits.
Ŝercoj ja havas limojn.

127 - 6

Friday would be perfect.
Vendredo estus perfekta.

127 - 7

I live in london.
Mi loĝas en londono.

Day 127

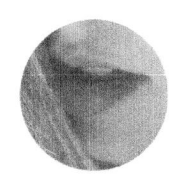

Week 19

128 - 1

Please keep quiet.
Bonvolu silenti.

128 - 2

Make a withdrawal.
Faru retiriĝon.

128 - 3

I was shocked to hear.
Mi ŝokis aŭdi.

128 - 4

My grandfather is well.
Mia avo fartas bone.

128 - 5

Do not wash.
Ne lavu.

128 - 6

I'm okay. thank you.
Mi fartas bone. dankon.

128 - 7

Why is the train late?
Kial la trajno malfruas?

Day 128

Week 19

129 - 1

What is your dress size?
Kio estas via vesta grandeco?

129 - 2

My car has broken down.
Mia aŭto paneis.

129 - 3

What day is it?
Kiu tago estas?

129 - 4

Fit as a fiddle.
Taŭga kiel fiolo.

129 - 5

No jumping.
Neniu saltado.

129 - 6

What brand is that?
Kiu marko estas tio?

129 - 7

The bill, please.
La fakturo, mi petas.

Day 129

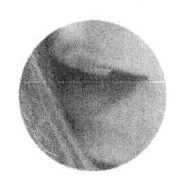

Week 19

130 - 1

Are you tired?
Ĉu vi lacas?

130 - 2

This is my brother.
Ĉi tiu estas mia frato.

130 - 3

Sounds great.
Sonas bonege.

130 - 4

A tube of toothpaste.
Tubo da dentopasto.

130 - 5

She smiled at me.
Ŝi ridetis al mi.

130 - 6

I don't have work today.
Mi ne havas laboron hodiaŭ.

130 - 7

Is he running?
Ĉu li kuras?

Day 130

LEARN ESPERANTO IN 52 WEEKS

LEARN ESPERANTO IN 52 WEEKS WITH 7 SENTENCES A DAY

Week 19

131 - 1

Have a safe trip back.
Havu sekuran vojaĝon reen.

131 - 2

He suddenly stood up.
Li subite ekstaris.

131 - 3

I like this.
Mi ŝatas tion ĉi.

19/52

131 - 4

I have a toothache.
Mi havas dentodoloron.

131 - 5

Do you know his name?
Ĉu vi konas lian nomon?

131 - 6

My back itches.
Mia dorso jukas.

131 - 7

I'm a terrible singer.
Mi estas terura kantisto.

Day 131

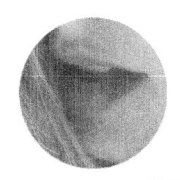

Week 19

132 - 1

Did you enjoy the meal?
Ĉu vi ĝuis la manĝon?

132 - 2

Let me help you.
Lasu min helpi vin.

132 - 3

We met yesterday.
Ni renkontiĝis hieraŭ.

132 - 4

Don't panic.
Ne paniku.

132 - 5

It's pouring.
Verŝas.

132 - 6

He laughed loudly.
Li laŭte ridis.

132 - 7

Can i leave a message?
Ĉu mi povas lasi mesaĝon?

Day 132

Test 19

133 - 1

Friday would be perfect.

133 - 2

Do not wash.

133 - 3

Fit as a fiddle.

133 - 4

Sounds great.

133 - 5

He suddenly stood up.

133 - 6

Did you enjoy the meal?

133 - 7

Can i leave a message?

Day 133

Week 20

134 - 1
Where is your house?
Kie estas via domo?

134 - 2
Return it safely.
Redonu ĝin sekure.

134 - 3
Welcome home.
Bonvenon hejmen.

134 - 4
I guarantee your safety.
Mi garantias vian sekurecon.

134 - 5
Now i've got to go.
Nun mi devas iri.

134 - 6
I mended it.
Mi riparis ĝin.

134 - 7
The skirt is too short.
La jupo estas tro mallonga.

Day 134

Week 20

135 - 1

May i offer you a drink?
Ĉu mi povas proponi al vi trinkaĵon?

135 - 2

Are you free now?
Ĉu vi nun estas libera?

135 - 3

I have no office today.
Mi ne havas oficejon hodiaŭ.

135 - 4

I'm hungry.
Mi estas malsata.

135 - 5

This is my boss.
Ĉi tiu estas mia estro.

135 - 6

Where's the bathroom?
Kie estas la banĉambro?

135 - 7

Where are my books?
Kie estas miaj libroj?

Day 135

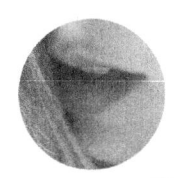

Week 20

136 - 1

I am always positive.
Mi ĉiam estas pozitiva.

136 - 2

This is my house.
Ĉi tiu estas mia domo.

136 - 3

I got sand in my shoes.
Mi ricevis sablon en miaj ŝuoj.

136 - 4

Don't do such a thing.
Ne faru tian aferon.

136 - 5

I hate onions.
Mi malamas cepojn.

136 - 6

He lost his girlfriend.
Li perdis sian amatinon.

136 - 7

He left the group.
Li forlasis la grupon.

Day 136

Week 20

137 - 1

Whose book is this?
Kies libro estas ĉi tiu?

137 - 2

Put out the fire.
Estingu la fajron.

137 - 3

What about a cup of tea?
Kio pri taso da teo?

20/52

137 - 4

I work as a doctor.
Mi laboras kiel kuracisto.

137 - 5

He finally showed up.
Li finfine aperis.

137 - 6

He's incapable.
Li estas nekapabla.

137 - 7

Julia is my sister.
Julia estas mia fratino.

Day 137

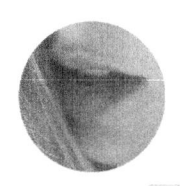

Week 20

138 - 1

Keep yourself cool.
Tenu vin malvarmeta.

138 - 2

How was your vacation?
Kiel estis via ferio?

138 - 3

I ate a lot of salad.
Mi manĝis multe da salato.

138 - 4

Sorry. you can't.
Pardonu. vi ne povas.

138 - 5

Do whatever you want.
Faru kion ajn vi volas.

138 - 6

I'm frightened.
Mi timas.

138 - 7

It was nice meeting you.
Estis agrable renkonti vin.

Day 138

Week 20

139 - 1

I don't eat salad.
Mi ne manĝas salaton.

139 - 2

We will have a meeting.
Ni havos kunvenon.

139 - 3

Nice day, isn't it?
Belan tagon, ĉu ne?

20/52

139 - 4

I'm sorry, i can't.
Pardonu, mi ne povas.

139 - 5

You're bleeding.
Vi sangas.

139 - 6

I go by train.
Mi iras per trajno.

139 - 7

Coffee is on the house.
Kafo estas sur la domo.

Day 139

Test 20

140 - 1

I mended it.

140 - 2

This is my boss.

140 - 3

Don't do such a thing.

20/52

140 - 4

What about a cup of tea?

140 - 5

How was your vacation?

140 - 6

I don't eat salad.

140 - 7

Coffee is on the house.

Day 140

Week 21

141 - 1

This whisky is strong.
Ĉi tiu viskio estas forta.

141 - 2

I have the flu.
Mi havas la gripon.

141 - 3

She is a bad woman.
Ŝi estas malbona virino.

141 - 4

This is a secret.
Ĉi tio estas sekreto.

141 - 5

He has my number.
Li havas mian numeron.

141 - 6

I uncorked the wine.
Mi malŝtopis la vinon.

141 - 7

It's too late now.
Estas tro malfrue nun.

Day 141

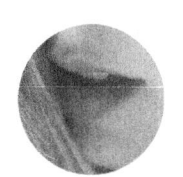

Week 21

142 - 1

He didn't work hard.
Li ne multe laboris.

142 - 2

How about you?
Kaj vi?

142 - 3

He came here alone.
Li venis ĉi tien sola.

142 - 4

When do you go to bed?
Kiam vi enlitiĝas?

142 - 5

May i have a fork?
Ĉu mi rajtas havi forkon?

142 - 6

I haven't decided yet.
Mi ankoraŭ ne decidis.

142 - 7

That's what i think too.
Tion ankaŭ mi pensas.

Day 142

Week 21

143 - 1

L feel sad today.
Mi sentas min malĝoja hodiaŭ.

143 - 2

Could you repeat?
Ĉu vi povus ripeti?

143 - 3

With pleasure.
Kun plezuro.

143 - 4

You're kidding.
Vi ŝercas.

143 - 5

I can't believe that.
Mi ne povas kredi tion.

143 - 6

Well done.
Bone farita.

143 - 7

Please stay as you are.
Bonvolu resti kiel vi estas.

Day 143

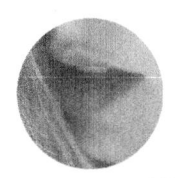

Week 21

144 - 1

I'm not interested.
Mi ne interesiĝas.

144 - 2

I pickup very fast.
Mi kaptas tre rapide.

144 - 3

I am out for lunch.
Mi estas ekstere por tagmanĝi.

21/52

144 - 4

Do you avoid me?
Ĉu vi evitas min?

144 - 5

Is he coming regularly?
Ĉu li venas regule?

144 - 6

He runs fast.
Li kuras rapide.

144 - 7

I tripped on a stone.
Mi stumblis sur ŝtono.

Day 144

Week 21

145 - 1

We can't do it here.
Ni ne povas fari ĝin ĉi tie.

145 - 2

Hold on tight.
Tenu forte.

145 - 3

Does he complain?
Ĉu li plendas?

145 - 4

What sizes do you have?
Kiajn grandecojn vi havas?

145 - 5

Is this book good?
Ĉu ĉi tiu libro estas bona?

145 - 6

That's wonderful.
Tio estas mirinda.

145 - 7

Are you good at tennis?
Ĉu vi lertas pri teniso?

Day 145

Week 21

146 - 1

Don't be too greedy.
Ne estu tro avida.

146 - 2

No trespassing here.
Nenia transpaso ĉi tie.

146 - 3

I'm not available today.
Mi ne disponeblas hodiaŭ.

146 - 4

Do you have a black pen?
Ĉu vi havas nigran plumon?

146 - 5

What does it mean?
Kion ĝi signifas?

146 - 6

I caught a cold.
Mi malvarmumis.

146 - 7

Are you afraid of them?
Ĉu vi timas ilin?

Day 146

Test 21

147 - 1

I uncorked the wine.

147 - 2

May i have a fork?

147 - 3

You're kidding.

147 - 4

I am out for lunch.

147 - 5

Hold on tight.

147 - 6

Don't be too greedy.

147 - 7

Are you afraid of them?

Day 147

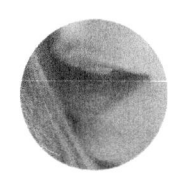

Week 22

148 - 1

He slipped on the snow.
Li glitis sur la neĝo.

148 - 2

I'm starving.
Mi malsategas.

148 - 3

The house is spacious.
La domo estas ampleksa.

148 - 4

I jog every morning.
Mi trotadas ĉiumatene.

148 - 5

How will you manage?
Kiel vi administros?

148 - 6

I work at a bank.
Mi laboras en banko.

148 - 7

He was very helpful.
Li estis tre helpema.

Day 148

Week 22

149 - 1

How sure are you?
Kiom certa vi estas?

149 - 2

He works hard every day.
Li laboras forte ĉiutage.

149 - 3

I slept well last night.
Mi dormis bone hieraŭ nokte.

149 - 4

I need some medicine.
Mi bezonas iom da medikamento.

149 - 5

We met on the internet.
Ni renkontis en la interreto.

149 - 6

What's your view?
Kio estas via opinio?

149 - 7

Everybody is fine.
Ĉiuj fartas bone.

Day 149

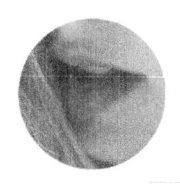

Week 22

150 - 1

Do you have a fever?
Ĉu vi havas febron?

150 - 2

I am sorry.
Mi bedaŭras.

150 - 3

That's ok.
Estas bone.

150 - 4

Are you not well?
Ĉu vi ne bone?

150 - 5

I'm feeling better.
Mi fartas pli bone.

150 - 6

This is absurd!
Ĉi tio estas absurda!

150 - 7

I have one brother.
Mi havas unu fraton.

Day 150

Week 22

151 - 1

He teaches mathematics.
Li instruas matematikon.

151 - 2

His grades went up.
Liaj notoj pliiĝis.

151 - 3

I am retired.
Mi estas emerita.

151 - 4

Will you be my friend?
Ĉu vi estos mia amiko?

151 - 5

This is my husband.
Ĉi tiu estas mia edzo.

151 - 6

Please speak slowly.
Bonvolu paroli malrapide.

151 - 7

I did it because of you.
Mi faris ĝin pro vi.

Day 151

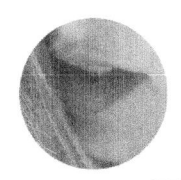

Week 22

152 - 1

Nice wearther, isn't it?
Bela portanto, ĉu ne?

152 - 2

I fed the dog.
Mi nutris la hundon.

152 - 3

He is out of town.
Li estas ekster la urbo.

152 - 4

This smells too sweet.
Ĉi tio odoras tro dolĉe.

152 - 5

Please bring the chair.
Bonvolu alporti la seĝon.

152 - 6

I have to go now.
Mi devas iri nun.

152 - 7

She's a busy person.
Ŝi estas okupata homo.

Day 152

Week 22

153 - 1

What happened?
Kio okazis?

153 - 2

I feel sleepy.
Mi sentas min dormema.

153 - 3

Don't talk about that.
Ne parolu pri tio.

153 - 4

The boss is coming.
La estro venas.

153 - 5

He's growing a beard.
Li kreskigas barbon.

153 - 6

For how many persons?
Por kiom da personoj?

153 - 7

Blue is your colour!
Blua estas via koloro!

Day 153

Test 22

154 - 1

I work at a bank.

154 - 2

We met on the internet.

154 - 3

Are you not well?

22/52

154 - 4

I am retired.

154 - 5

I fed the dog.

154 - 6

What happened?

154 - 7

Blue is your colour!

Day 154

Week 23

155 - 1

It's a fair way away.
Estas justa for.

155 - 2

My mother's a nurse.
Mia patrino estas flegistino.

155 - 3

I feel thirsty.
Mi sentas soifon.

155 - 4

This flower smells good.
Ĉi tiu floro bone odoras.

155 - 5

Hello, can you hear me?
Saluton, ĉu vi aŭdas min?

155 - 6

How are you?
Kiel vi fartas?

155 - 7

Don't go near him!
Ne alproksimiĝu al li!

Day 155

Week 23

156 - 1

You can do it!
Vi povas fari ĝin!

156 - 2

It's too loose for me.
Ĝi estas tro malfiksa por mi.

156 - 3

I work in healthcare.
Mi laboras en sanservo.

156 - 4

His business failed.
Lia komerco malsukcesis.

156 - 5

He's a nice guy.
Li estas simpatia ulo.

156 - 6

He spat on the ground.
Li kraĉis sur la teron.

156 - 7

My soup is cold.
Mia supo estas malvarma.

Day 156

Week 23

157 - 1

What station is it?
Kiu stacio estas?

157 - 2

She can speak italian.
Ŝi scipovas paroli la italan.

157 - 3

I'm in charge of sales.
Mi respondecas pri vendoj.

157 - 4

He is an unlikable man.
Li estas malŝatata viro.

157 - 5

Do you have a sister?
Ĉu vi havas fratinon?

157 - 6

It's pouring down.
Verŝas malsupren.

157 - 7

I am outspoken.
Mi estas sincera.

Day 157

Week 23

158 - 1

Meet me tomorrow.
Renkontu min morgaŭ.

158 - 2

A double bed, please.
Duobla lito, mi petas.

158 - 3

Switch off the t.v.
Malŝaltu la t.v.

158 - 4

Excuse me.
Pardonu min.

158 - 5

I want to be a doctor.
Mi volas esti kuracisto.

158 - 6

Yes, i am certain.
Jes, mi estas certa.

158 - 7

I love summer.
Mi amas someron.

Day 158

Week 23

159 - 1

The exam was difficult.
La ekzameno estis malfacila.

159 - 2

You're right.
Vi pravas.

159 - 3

I got wet in the rain.
Mi malsekiĝis en la pluvo.

159 - 4

Please do.
Bonvolu fari.

159 - 5

I haven't tried it on.
Mi ne provis ĝin.

159 - 6

Do not lose your ticket.
Ne perdu vian bileton.

159 - 7

How much does it cost?
Kiom ĝi kostas?

Day 159

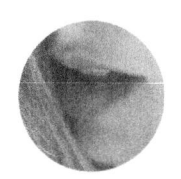

Week 23

160 - 1

That's a good idea.
Tio estas bona ideo.

160 - 2

Sure. thank you.
Certe. dankon.

160 - 3

It is nothing.
Estas nenio.

160 - 4

This dance is easy.
Ĉi tiu danco estas facila.

160 - 5

I moved last year.
Mi translokiĝis pasintjare.

160 - 6

See you soon.
Ĝis baldaŭ.

160 - 7

She is not that stupid.
Ŝi ne estas tiel stulta.

Day 160

Test 23

161 - 1

How are you?

161 - 2

He's a nice guy.

161 - 3

He is an unlikable man.

161 - 4

Switch off the t.v.

161 - 5

You're right.

161 - 6

That's a good idea.

161 - 7

She is not that stupid.

Day 161

Week 24

162 - 1

What do you suggest?
Kion vi proponas?

162 - 2

Do you have any idea?
Ĉu vi havas ideon?

162 - 3

I'm working as a waiter.
Mi laboras kiel kelnero.

162 - 4

My stomach hurts a lot.
Mia stomako multe doloras.

162 - 5

Slow down.
Malrapidiĝu.

162 - 6

It was a foggy night.
Estis nebula nokto.

162 - 7

It's time for lunch.
Estas tempo por tagmanĝi.

Day 162

Week 24

163 - 1

I am so stressed.
Mi estas tiel streĉita.

163 - 2

Listen to your body.
Aŭskultu vian korpon.

163 - 3

You're special to me.
Vi estas speciala por mi.

163 - 4

Happy anniversary!
Feliĉan datrevenon!

163 - 5

I had a great time.
Mi havis bonegan tempon.

163 - 6

What do you see?
Kion vi vidas?

163 - 7

It was pouring today.
Verŝiĝis hodiaŭ.

Day 163

Week 24

164 - 1

I don't care.
Mi ne zorgas.

164 - 2

Is service included?
Ĉu servo inkluzivas?

164 - 3

I have no change.
Mi ne havas ŝanĝon.

164 - 4

Well, shall we go?
Nu, ĉu ni iru?

164 - 5

It's time to leave.
Estas tempo foriri.

164 - 6

Does he add wealth?
Ĉu li aldonas riĉaĵon?

164 - 7

It's too long.
Ĝi estas tro longa.

Day 164

Week 24

165 - 1

You are all set.
Vi estas tute preta.

165 - 2

Take a deep breath.
Enspiru profunde.

165 - 3

People speak french.
Homoj parolas la francan.

165 - 4

It's too long for me.
Estas tro longa por mi.

165 - 5

It's too small for me.
Ĝi estas tro malgranda por mi.

165 - 6

Is the seat vacant?
Ĉu la sidloko estas libera?

165 - 7

He is busy as usual.
Li estas okupata kiel kutime.

Day 165

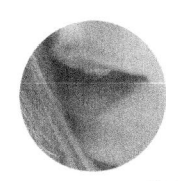

Week 24

166 - 1

Can i travel?
Ĉu mi povas vojaĝi?

166 - 2

Here you go.
Jen.

166 - 3

He's rich.
Li estas riĉa.

166 - 4

How about water?
Kio pri akvo?

166 - 5

Be quiet as you leave.
Estu silenta dum vi foriras.

166 - 6

I like oranges.
Mi ŝatas oranĝojn.

166 - 7

Don't try my patience.
Ne provu mian paciencon.

Day 166

Week 24

167 - 1

I love you.
Mi amas vin.

167 - 2

He is in debt.
Li estas en ŝuldo.

167 - 3

He's a loser.
Li estas malgajninto.

167 - 4

I'll ride there.
Mi rajdos tien.

167 - 5

He ate rice in a bowl.
Li manĝis rizon en bovlo.

167 - 6

How did you get there?
Kiel vi alvenis tie?

167 - 7

I don't feel like it.
Mi ne emas.

Day 167

Test 24

168 - 1

It was a foggy night.

168 - 2

I had a great time.

168 - 3

Well, shall we go?

168 - 4

People speak french.

168 - 5

Here you go.

168 - 6

I love you.

168 - 7

I don't feel like it.

Day 168

LEARN ESPERANTO IN 52 WEEKS

LEARN ESPERANTO IN 52 WEEKS WITH 7 SENTENCES A DAY

Week 25

169 - 1

I want new shoes.
Mi volas novajn ŝuojn.

169 - 2

Thanks for calling.
Dankon pro voko.

169 - 3

I will call for help.
Mi vokos por helpo.

25/52

169 - 4

He'll come after lunch.
Li venos post tagmanĝo.

169 - 5

Thank you very much.
Dankegon.

169 - 6

Do you have insurance?
Ĉu vi havas asekuron?

169 - 7

Nice work.
Bela laboro.

Day 169

Week 25

170 - 1

This is a true story.
Ĉi tio estas vera rakonto.

170 - 2

I left a key with him.
Mi lasis ŝlosilon ĉe li.

170 - 3

When will he be back?
Kiam li revenos?

170 - 4

I don't think so.
Mi ne pensas tiel.

170 - 5

I chilled beer.
Mi malvarmigis bieron.

170 - 6

Where do you live?
Kie vi loĝas?

170 - 7

Did you pass the exam?
Ĉu vi trapasis la ekzamenon?

Day 170

Week 25

171 - 1

Is that seat available?
Ĉu tiu sidloko disponeblas?

171 - 2

I hate ironing.
Mi malamas gladi.

171 - 3

Are they from abroad?
Ĉu ili estas eksterlandaj?

171 - 4

Is it raining?
Ĉu pluvas?

171 - 5

Don't beat him.
Ne batu lin.

171 - 6

What time is checkout?
Je kioma horo estas checkout?

171 - 7

Are you going with them?
Ĉu vi iras kun ili?

Day 171

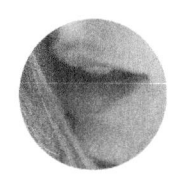

Week 25

172 - 1

What a bad idea.
Kia malbona ideo.

172 - 2

I will consult my boss.
Mi konsultos mian estron.

172 - 3

He loves barbecues.
Li amas kradrostojn.

172 - 4

The house is lovely.
La domo estas ĉarma.

172 - 5

Is he breathing?
Ĉu li spiras?

172 - 6

I run my own business.
Mi administras mian propran komercon.

172 - 7

Don't waste my time.
Ne malŝparu mian tempon.

Day 172

Week 25

173 - 1

Why didn't you come?
Kial vi ne venis?

173 - 2

I would rather go home.
Mi preferus iri hejmen.

173 - 3

He's already gone home.
Li jam iris hejmen.

173 - 4

Did she appeal?
Ĉu ŝi apelaciis?

173 - 5

It smells good.
Ĝi odoras bone.

173 - 6

He gulped down water.
Li englutis akvon.

173 - 7

That pond is very deep.
Tiu lageto estas tre profunda.

Day 173

Week 25

174 - 1

When were you born?
Kiam vi naskiĝis?

174 - 2

Sure. i'll come.
Certe. mi venos.

174 - 3

I have made a mistake.
Mi faris eraron.

174 - 4

Please ask someone.
Bonvolu demandi iun.

174 - 5

Pretty well.
Sufiĉe bone.

174 - 6

You're hired.
Vi estas dungita.

174 - 7

My mother was crying.
Mia patrino ploris.

Day 174

Test 25

175 - 1

Do you have insurance?

175 - 2

I chilled beer.

175 - 3

Is it raining?

175 - 4

He loves barbecues.

175 - 5

I would rather go home.

175 - 6

When were you born?

175 - 7

My mother was crying.

Day 175

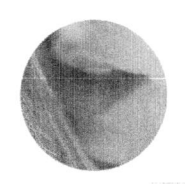

Week 26

176 - 1

The floor is slippery.
La planko estas glitiga.

176 - 2

You can go home.
Vi povas iri hejmen.

176 - 3

Please have your seat.
Bonvolu havi vian sidlokon.

176 - 4

No smoking.
Ne fumi.

176 - 5

It's warm.
Estas varme.

176 - 6

Good afternoon.
Bonan posttagmezon.

176 - 7

I'm in a lot of pain.
Mi multe suferas.

Day 176

LEARN ESPERANTO IN 52 WEEKS

LEARN ESPERANTO IN 52 WEEKS WITH 7 SENTENCES A DAY

Week 26

177 - 1

This bra is too small.
Ĉi tiu mamzono estas tro malgranda.

177 - 2

How's your day?
Kiel fartas via tago?

177 - 3

How tall is that tower?
Kiom altas tiu turo?

177 - 4

Do not stare at people.
Ne rigardu homojn.

26/52

177 - 5

With whom did you come?
Kun kiu vi venis?

177 - 6

Wear your life guards.
Portu viajn savgardistojn.

177 - 7

Use black ink only.
Uzu nur nigran inkon.

Day 177

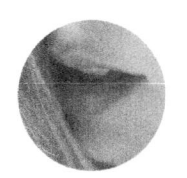

Week 26

178 - 1

Find the value of x.
Trovu la valoron de x.

178 - 2

Did he borrow a pen?
Ĉu li pruntis plumon?

178 - 3

Enjoy your stay!
Ĝuu vian restadon!

178 - 4

This is my sister.
Ĉi tiu estas mia fratino.

178 - 5

I sat in a window seat.
Mi sidis en fenestra seĝo.

178 - 6

I'm afraid not.
Mi timas, ke ne.

178 - 7

This is a great chance.
Ĉi tio estas bonega ŝanco.

Day 178

Week 26

179 - 1

He's short.
Li estas malalta.

179 - 2

There is an accident.
Estas akcidento.

179 - 3

Is this seat taken?
Ĉu ĉi tiu sidloko estas prenita?

179 - 4

Traffic light ahead.
Semaforo antaŭen.

179 - 5

Let's ask mom.
Ni demandu panjon.

179 - 6

I am a computer analyst.
Mi estas komputila analizisto.

179 - 7

Her words hurt me.
Ŝiaj vortoj dolorigis min.

Day 179

Week 26

180 - 1

It might rain today.
Eble pluvos hodiaŭ.

180 - 2

Did you type the letter?
Ĉu vi tajpis la leteron?

180 - 3

I'm off on thursday.
Mi foriras ĵaŭdon.

180 - 4

Focus on your goal.
Koncentru vian celon.

180 - 5

His legs are short.
Liaj kruroj estas mallongaj.

180 - 6

How are you doing?
Kiel vi fartas?

180 - 7

His driving is awful.
Lia veturado estas terura.

Day 180

Week 26

181 - 1

She's studying drama.
Ŝi studas dramon.

181 - 2

We got on the ship.
Ni eniris la ŝipon.

181 - 3

I love dogs.
Mi amas hundojn.

181 - 4

Great, thanks.
Bonege, dankon.

181 - 5

She was quiet at first.
Ŝi estis kvieta komence.

181 - 6

Why did he come here?
Kial li venis ĉi tien?

181 - 7

The light is still on.
La lumo ankoraŭ estas ŝaltita.

Day 181

Test 26

182 - 1

Good afternoon.

182 - 2

With whom did you come?

182 - 3

This is my sister.

182 - 4

Is this seat taken?

182 - 5

Did you type the letter?

182 - 6

She's studying drama.

182 - 7

The light is still on.

Day 182

LEARN ESPERANTO IN 52 WEEKS

LEARN ESPERANTO IN 52 WEEKS WITH 7 SENTENCES A DAY

Week 27

183 - 1

Can we meet next friday?
Ĉu ni povas renkontiĝi la venontan vendredon?

183 - 2

I eat bread every day.
Mi manĝas panon ĉiutage.

183 - 3

What is your dream job?
Kio estas via revo laboron?

183 - 4

Hello! do come in!
Saluton! eniru!

183 - 5

When is he returning?
Kiam li revenas?

183 - 6

I can't help you.
Mi ne povas helpi vin.

183 - 7

A kilo of fish.
Kilo da fiŝo.

Day 183

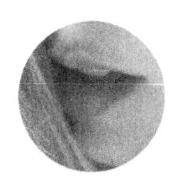

Week 27

184 - 1

How was your day?
Kiel estis via tago?

184 - 2

Please breathe slowly.
Bonvolu spiri malrapide.

184 - 3

I have no money.
Mi ne havas monon.

184 - 4

What are your symptoms?
Kiuj estas viaj simptomoj?

184 - 5

I'd be happy to.
Mi ĝojus.

184 - 6

Nobody can replace him.
Neniu povas anstataŭigi lin.

184 - 7

A slice of pizza.
Trançajo da pico.

Day 184

Week 27

185 - 1

Let's go over there.
Ni iru tien.

185 - 2

I like this bag.
Mi ŝatas ĉi tiun sakon.

185 - 3

I am in pain.
Mi suferas.

185 - 4

When is your birthday?
Kiam estas via naskiĝtago?

185 - 5

I read your book.
Mi legis vian libron.

185 - 6

I doubt it.
Mi dubas pri tio.

185 - 7

Your guest has arrived.
Via gasto alvenis.

Day 185

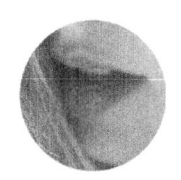

Week 27

186 - 1

I keep my promise.
Mi plenumas mian promeson.

186 - 2

Of course.
Kompreneble.

186 - 3

I have a black bag.
Mi havas nigran sakon.

186 - 4

I love my job.
Mi amas mian laboron.

186 - 5

You need to swipe it.
Vi devas gliti ĝin.

186 - 6

It's five to five.
Estas kvin ĝis kvin.

186 - 7

I don't like crowds.
Mi ne ŝatas homamasojn.

Day 186

Week 27

187 - 1

No big thing.
Neniu granda afero.

187 - 2

Have you got a computer?
Ĉu vi havas komputilon?

187 - 3

I'm not good at math.
Mi ne lertas pri matematiko.

187 - 4

He studies medicine.
Li studas medicinon.

187 - 5

It rained yesterday.
Pluvis hieraŭ.

187 - 6

Does she behold me?
Ĉu ŝi rigardas min?

187 - 7

It hurts.
Doloras.

Day 187

Week 27

188 - 1

My specialty is law.
Mia fako estas juro.

188 - 2

A table for two, please.
Tablo por du, mi petas.

188 - 3

Sorry for my fault.
Pardonu pro mia kulpo.

188 - 4

Yes. certainly.
Jes. certe.

188 - 5

Read your books quietly.
Legu viajn librojn kviete.

188 - 6

Let's talk calmly.
Ni parolu trankvile.

188 - 7

Please open to page 32.
Bonvolu malfermi al paĝo 32.

Day 188

Test 27

189 - 1

I can't help you.

189 - 2

I'd be happy to.

189 - 3

When is your birthday?

189 - 4

I have a black bag.

189 - 5

Have you got a computer?

189 - 6

My specialty is law.

189 - 7

Please open to page 32.

Day 189

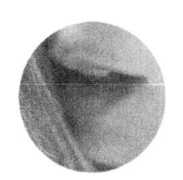

Week 28

190 - 1

His crime is serious.
Lia krimo estas grava.

190 - 2

I belong to chicago.
Mi apartenas al ĉikago.

190 - 3

She has special powers.
Ŝi havas specialajn potencojn.

190 - 4

Is he a teacher?
Ĉu li estas instruisto?

28/52

190 - 5

It's for a present.
Ĝi estas por donaco.

190 - 6

It's midnight.
Estas noktomezo.

190 - 7

I'll go there by bus.
Mi iros tien per buso.

Day 190

Week 28

191 - 1

Please turn left there.
Bonvolu turni maldekstren tie.

191 - 2

He is on leave.
Li estas en forpermeso.

191 - 3

He's a good person.
Li estas bona homo.

191 - 4

No stopping.
Neniu halto.

28/52

191 - 5

Can i help you?
Ĉu mi povas helpi vin?

191 - 6

Too bad.
Tro malbone.

191 - 7

I paid my car tax.
Mi pagis mian aŭto-imposton.

Day 191

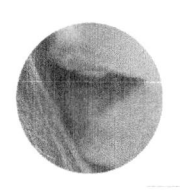

Week 28

192 - 1

This cup is plastic.
Ĉi tiu taso estas plasta.

192 - 2

He's off-guard.
Li estas sengarda.

192 - 3

Is it all true?
Ĉu ĉio estas vera?

192 - 4

It is very cold.
Estas tre malvarme.

192 - 5

Everyone makes mistakes.
Ĉiuj faras erarojn.

192 - 6

What a beautiful sunset!
Kia bela sunsubiro!

192 - 7

Is the shop open?
Ĉu la butiko estas malfermita?

Day 192

Week 28

193 - 1

He is my best friend.
Li estas mia plej bona amiko.

193 - 2

She cried out for help.
Ŝi kriis por helpo.

193 - 3

You deserve it!
Vi meritas tion!

193 - 4

I swam a lot yesterday.
Mi multe naĝis hieraŭ.

193 - 5

I left her a message.
Mi lasis al ŝi mesaĝon.

193 - 6

He has thick eyebrows.
Li havas dikajn brovojn.

193 - 7

I am fine and you?
Mi fartas bone kaj vi?

Day 193

Week 28

194 - 1

I'm 27 years old.
Mi aĝas 27 jarojn.

194 - 2

A woman approached me.
Virino alproksimiĝis al mi.

194 - 3

It looks delicious.
Ĝi aspektas bongusta.

194 - 4

I will take a bath.
Mi baniĝos.

194 - 5

How disappointing.
Kiel seniluziiga.

194 - 6

It tastes good!
Ĝi bongustas!

194 - 7

Can i give you a hand?
Ĉu mi povas doni al vi manon?

Day 194

Week 28

195 - 1

He knows my number.
Li konas mian numeron.

195 - 2

Close the door properly.
Fermu la pordon ĝuste.

195 - 3

He injured his elbow.
Li vundis sian kubuton.

195 - 4

Who is still answering?
Kiu ankoraŭ respondas?

195 - 5

I need to get a job.
Mi bezonas akiri laboron.

195 - 6

Do you understand?
Ĉu vi komprenas?

195 - 7

This pillow is too low.
Ĉi tiu kuseno estas tro malalta.

Day 195

Test 28

196 - 1

It's midnight.

196 - 2

Can i help you?

196 - 3

It is very cold.

196 - 4

You deserve it!

28/52

196 - 5

A woman approached me.

196 - 6

He knows my number.

196 - 7

This pillow is too low.

Day 196

Week 29

197 - 1

He came by bus.
Li venis per buso.

197 - 2

This cake is yummy.
Ĉi tiu kuko estas bongusta.

197 - 3

I will never forget you.
Mi neniam forgesos vin.

197 - 4

He is doing fine.
Li fartas bone.

197 - 5

How is your brother?
Kiel fartas via frato?

197 - 6

This is a shortcut.
Ĉi tio estas ŝparvojo.

197 - 7

Maximum occupancy.
Maksimuma okupado.

Day 197

Week 29

198 - 1

You look great.
Vi aspektas bonege.

198 - 2

Who will help you?
Kiu helpos vin?

198 - 3

Don't move with them.
Ne moviĝu kun ili.

198 - 4

The diamond glittered.
La diamanto brilis.

198 - 5

It's ten past eleven.
Estas la deka post la dekunua.

198 - 6

Are you on time?
Ĉu vi estas ĝustatempe?

198 - 7

The house is big.
La domo estas granda.

Day 198

LEARN ESPERANTO IN 52 WEEKS

LEARN ESPERANTO IN 52 WEEKS WITH 7 SENTENCES A DAY

Week 29

199 - 1

I come from chicago.
Mi venas el ĉikago.

199 - 2

Are you married?
Ĉu vi estas edziĝinta?

199 - 3

Best of luck.
Bonŝancon.

199 - 4

Lastly, you.
Laste, vi.

29/52

199 - 5

Life in spain is fun.
La vivo en hispanio estas amuza.

199 - 6

How is your father?
Kiel fartas via patro?

199 - 7

Please give an example.
Bonvolu doni ekzemplon.

Day 199

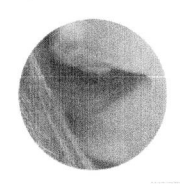

Week 29

200 - 1

His voice is soft.
Lia voĉo estas milda.

200 - 2

The team was weak.
La teamo estis malforta.

200 - 3

Which one is the sauce?
Kiu estas la saŭco?

200 - 4

Remind me.
Memorigi min.

200 - 5

Eat slowly.
Manĝu malrapide.

200 - 6

They are engaged.
Ili estas fianĉigitaj.

200 - 7

The movie opens today.
La filmo malfermiĝas hodiaŭ.

Day 200

LEARN ESPERANTO IN 52 WEEKS

LEARN ESPERANTO IN 52 WEEKS WITH 7 SENTENCES A DAY

Week 29

201 - 1

I have my own business.
Mi havas mian propran komercon.

201 - 2

I'm learning judo.
Mi lernas ĵudon.

201 - 3

Drink your coffee.
Trinku vian kafon.

201 - 4

Violence is wrong.
Perforto estas malĝusta.

29/52

201 - 5

Please call a taxi.
Bonvolu voki taksion.

201 - 6

Did you call me?
Ĉu vi vokis min?

201 - 7

Where do you come from?
Kie vi venis?

Day 201

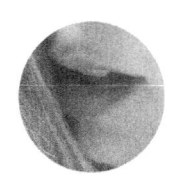

Week 29

202 - 1

He denied the rumor.
Li neis la onidiron.

202 - 2

Don't act recklessly.
Ne agu malprudente.

202 - 3

My son is now a toddler.
Mia filo nun estas infaneto.

202 - 4

Will it rain today?
Ĉu pluvos hodiaŭ?

202 - 5

Solve the equation.
Solvu la ekvacion.

202 - 6

Here is your key.
Jen via ŝlosilo.

202 - 7

Can i sit here?
Ĉu mi povas sidi ĉi tie?

Day 202

Test 29

203 - 1

This is a shortcut.

203 - 2

It's ten past eleven.

203 - 3

Lastly, you.

203 - 4

Which one is the sauce?

203 - 5

I'm learning judo.

203 - 6

He denied the rumor.

203 - 7

Can i sit here?

Day 203

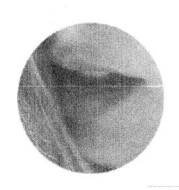

Week 30

204 - 1

A pinch of salt.
Pinĉo da salo.

204 - 2

She rarely gets angry.
Ŝi malofte koleriĝas.

204 - 3

Help! shark attack!
Helpu! ŝarka atako!

204 - 4

Please take notes.
Bonvolu preni notojn.

204 - 5

Your skirt is rumpled.
Via jupo estas ĉifita.

204 - 6

What should i do?
Kion mi devus fari?

204 - 7

He sold the house.
Li vendis la domon.

Day 204

Week 30

205 - 1

Is she your sister?
Ĉu ŝi estas via fratino?

205 - 2

She's always smiling.
Ŝi ĉiam ridetas.

205 - 3

She ironed the shirt.
Ŝi gladis la ĉemizon.

205 - 4

She's a gorgeous woman.
Ŝi estas belega virino.

205 - 5

My head aches.
Mia kapo doloras.

205 - 6

His movements are quick.
Liaj movoj estas rapidaj.

205 - 7

Is he your relative?
Ĉu li estas via parenco?

Day 205

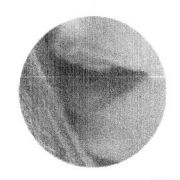

Week 30

206 - 1

Hello everyone.
Saluton al ĉiuj.

206 - 2

Why did he come?
Kial li venis?

206 - 3

It's nice out today.
Estas agrable ekstere hodiaŭ.

206 - 4

Actually, i like her.
Efektive, mi ŝatas ŝin.

206 - 5

Sorry to say that.
Pardonu diri tion.

206 - 6

I will try this.
Mi provos ĉi tion.

206 - 7

I'll be online.
Mi estos enreta.

Day 206

Week 30

207 - 1

I hope they will win.
Mi esperas, ke ili venkos.

207 - 2

May i have your address?
Ĉu mi rajtas havi vian adreson?

207 - 3

It's very gaudy.
Ĝi estas tre okulfrapa.

207 - 4

My nose is itchy.
Mia nazo jukas.

207 - 5

Please turn this way.
Bonvolu turni sin ĉi tien.

207 - 6

She's greedy.
Ŝi estas avida.

207 - 7

It's a great shame.
Estas granda honto.

Day 207

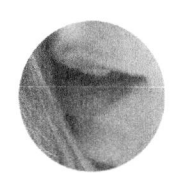

Week 30

208 - 1

He turned on the tap.
Li malfermis la kranon.

208 - 2

She was very brave.
Ŝi estis tre kuraĝa.

208 - 3

The dog bit my hand.
La hundo mordis mian manon.

208 - 4

I hate cigarettes.
Mi malamas cigaredojn.

208 - 5

My watch is slow.
Mia horloĝo estas malrapida.

208 - 6

It's cloudy today.
Estas nuba hodiaŭ.

208 - 7

It's always lively here.
Ĉi tie estas ĉiam vigla.

Day 208

Week 30

209 - 1

Her baby is cute.
Ŝia bebo estas ĉarma.

209 - 2

It looks great on you!
Ĝi aspektas bonege ĉe vi!

209 - 3

Insert card here.
Enigu karton ĉi tie.

209 - 4

Certainly.
Certe.

209 - 5

I am on a business trip.
Mi estas en komerca vojaĝo.

209 - 6

I need to see a doctor.
Mi devas vidi kuraciston.

209 - 7

Roses smell sweet.
Rozoj odoras dolĉe.

Day 209

LEARN ESPERANTO IN 52 WEEKS

LEARN ESPERANTO IN 52 WEEKS WITH 7 SENTENCES A DAY

Test 30

210 - 1

What should i do?

210 - 2

My head aches.

210 - 3

Actually, i like her.

210 - 4

It's very gaudy.

210 - 5

She was very brave.

210 - 6

Her baby is cute.

210 - 7

Roses smell sweet.

Day 210

Week 31

211 - 1

Is he giving the book?
Ĉu li donas la libron?

211 - 2

My nails have grown.
Miaj ungoj kreskis.

211 - 3

Safe trip!
Sekura vojaĝo!

211 - 4

What is wrong with you?
Kio estas en vi?

211 - 5

That's fine.
Tio estas bone.

211 - 6

I'm scared of dogs.
Mi timas hundojn.

211 - 7

Don't worry about it.
Ne zorgu pri tio.

Day 211

LEARN ESPERANTO IN 52 WEEKS
LEARN ESPERANTO IN 52 WEEKS WITH 7 SENTENCES A DAY

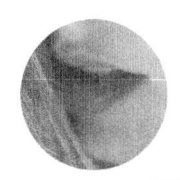

Week 31

212 - 1
Does he beat me?
Ĉu li batas min?

212 - 2
I am a teacher.
Mi estas instruisto.

212 - 3
She has a car.
Ŝi havas aŭton.

212 - 4
You couldn't do that.
Vi ne povis fari tion.

212 - 5
May i have a word?
Ĉu mi rajtas havi vorton?

212 - 6
Just a moment.
Nur momenton.

212 - 7
John, this is mary.
John, ĉi tiu estas maria.

Day 212

Week 31

213 - 1

Here is my passport.
Jen mia pasporto.

213 - 2

Please calm down.
Bonvolu trankviliĝi.

213 - 3

I'm scared of snakes.
Mi timas serpentojn.

213 - 4

Say cheese!
Diru fromaĝon!

213 - 5

The time now is 6:35.
La tempo nun estas 6:35.

213 - 6

He is a business man.
Li estas komercisto.

213 - 7

I was locked up.
Mi estis enŝlosita.

Day 213

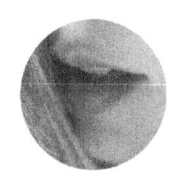

Week 31

214 - 1

We studied democracy.
Ni studis demokration.

214 - 2

How can i get there?
Kiel mi povas atingi tien?

214 - 3

The stew burnt.
La stufaĵo brulis.

214 - 4

How old is he?
Kiom li aĝas?

214 - 5

He mumbled to himself.
Li murmuris al si.

214 - 6

Sincerely thanks.
Elkore dankon.

214 - 7

Is this your bag?
Ĉu ĉi tio estas via sako?

Day 214

Week 31

215 - 1

Watch your mouth.
Gardu vian buŝon.

215 - 2

How old is the victim?
Kiom aĝas la viktimo?

215 - 3

His fingers are big.
Liaj fingroj estas grandaj.

215 - 4

He is a good cook.
Li estas bona kuiristo.

215 - 5

Please move forward.
Bonvolu antaŭeniri.

215 - 6

What's the matter?
Kio estas la problemo?

215 - 7

Please call back later.
Bonvolu retelefoni poste.

Day 215

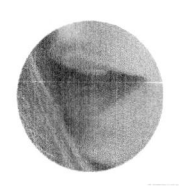

Week 31

216 - 1

I have a headache.
Mi havas kapdoloron.

216 - 2

It's very cold outside.
Estas tre malvarme ekstere.

216 - 3

It's pay day!
Estas salajrotago!

216 - 4

He works at an embassy.
Li laboras en ambasado.

216 - 5

I am living in london.
Mi loĝas en londono.

216 - 6

He plays the guitar.
Li ludas la gitaron.

216 - 7

Take a look around.
Rigardu ĉirkaŭen.

Day 216

Test 31

217 - 1
I'm scared of dogs.

217 - 2
May i have a word?

217 - 3
Say cheese!

217 - 4
The stew burnt.

217 - 5
How old is the victim?

217 - 6
I have a headache.

217 - 7
Take a look around.

Day 217

Week 32

218 - 1

I have little money.
Mi havas malmulte da mono.

218 - 2

Let me pour you a drink.
Lasu min verŝi al vi trinkaĵon.

218 - 3

She gripped my hand.
Ŝi kaptis mian manon.

218 - 4

I'll pay by card.
Mi pagos per karto.

218 - 5

He has a clean image.
Li havas puran bildon.

218 - 6

What's new?
Kio novas?

218 - 7

Where do you work?
Kie vi laboras?

Day 218

Week 32

219 - 1

I am a nurse.
Mi estas flegistino.

219 - 2

I forgave him.
Mi pardonis lin.

219 - 3

You may now go.
Vi nun povas iri.

219 - 4

He has weekdays off.
Li havas libertagojn.

219 - 5

What's your question?
Kio estas via demando?

219 - 6

They often play tennis.
Ili ofte ludas tenison.

219 - 7

That's alright.
Tio estas en ordo.

Day 219

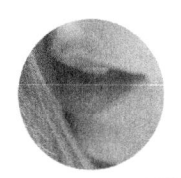

Week 32

220 - 1

3 is an odd number.
3 estas nepara nombro.

220 - 2

My jaw hurts.
Mia makzelo doloras.

220 - 3

Is he paying the fee?
Ĉu li pagas la kotizon?

220 - 4

Let's bring some water.
Ni alportu iom da akvo.

220 - 5

What a beautiful person!
Kia bela homo!

220 - 6

Make a note of it.
Notu ĝin.

220 - 7

Don't deceive people.
Ne trompu homojn.

Day 220

Week 32

221 - 1

I caught a butterfly.
Mi kaptis papilion.

221 - 2

He's courageous.
Li estas kuraĝa.

221 - 3

He believes in god.
Li kredas je dio.

221 - 4

I can't. i'm sorry.
Mi ne povas. mi bedaŭras.

221 - 5

Can i get extra linen?
Ĉu mi povas akiri kroman tolaĵon?

221 - 6

She refused to attend.
Ŝi rifuzis ĉeesti.

221 - 7

I'll be back.
Mi revenos.

Day 221

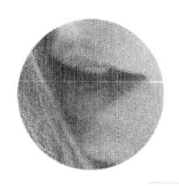

Week 32

222 - 1

Good luck to you.
Bonŝancon al vi.

222 - 2

He tried an experiment.
Li provis eksperimenton.

222 - 3

I'm positive.
Mi estas pozitiva.

222 - 4

My father drives safely.
Mia patro veturas sekure.

222 - 5

Talk to a witness.
Parolu kun atestanto.

222 - 6

This river is shallow.
Ĉi tiu rivero estas malprofunda.

222 - 7

No food and drinks.
Neniuj manĝaĵoj kaj trinkaĵoj.

Day 222

Week 32

223 - 1

Here is the bill.
Jen la fakturo.

223 - 2

I write right-handed.
Mi skribas dekstre.

223 - 3

How can i help you?
Kiel mi povas helpi vin?

223 - 4

It's hot outside.
Estas varme ekstere.

223 - 5

I'll take them all.
Mi prenos ilin ĉiujn.

223 - 6

He's very expressive.
Li estas tre esprimplena.

223 - 7

I don't need a bag.
Mi ne bezonas sakon.

Day 223

Test 32

224 - 1

What's new?

224 - 2

What's your question?

224 - 3

Let's bring some water.

224 - 4

He believes in god.

224 - 5

He tried an experiment.

224 - 6

Here is the bill.

224 - 7

I don't need a bag.

Day 224

Week 33

225 - 1

Don't play on the road.
Ne ludu sur la vojo.

225 - 2

We have to work on it.
Ni devas labori pri ĝi.

225 - 3

Why are you laughing?
Kial vi ridas?

225 - 4

I'll connect you now.
Mi konektos vin nun.

225 - 5

Close your eyes.
Fermu viajn okulojn.

225 - 6

It's very hot today.
Estas tre varme hodiaŭ.

225 - 7

She is my elder sister.
Ŝi estas mia pli aĝa fratino.

Day 225

Week 33

226 - 1

Do not drink.
Ne trinku.

226 - 2

I'll give you this book.
Mi donos al vi ĉi tiun libron.

226 - 3

I have a favor to ask.
Mi havas favoron por peti.

226 - 4

Put on your boots!
Surmetu viajn botojn!

226 - 5

The sun is glaring.
La suno brilas.

226 - 6

My friend got divorced.
Mia amiko eksedziĝis.

226 - 7

I have two brothers.
Mi havas du fratojn.

Day 226

Week 33

227 - 1

The steak here is ok.
La bifsteko ĉi tie estas en ordo.

227 - 2

I put butter in curry.
Mi metis buteron en kareon.

227 - 3

How many hours drive?
Kiom da horoj veturi?

227 - 4

His grades are not bad.
Liaj notoj ne estas malbonaj.

227 - 5

Does the sun appear?
Ĉu la suno aperas?

227 - 6

He rides a motorcycle.
Li veturas per motorciklo.

227 - 7

Please show me.
Bonvolu montri al mi.

Day 227

Week 33

228 - 1

I'm finished.
Mi estas finita.

228 - 2

Why did you go there?
Kial vi iris tien?

228 - 3

I have strong teeth.
Mi havas fortajn dentojn.

228 - 4

I'm looking for my dog.
Mi serĉas mian hundon.

228 - 5

Good luck.
Bonŝancon.

228 - 6

Then, you.
Tiam vi.

228 - 7

Please take me along.
Bonvolu kunporti min.

Day 228

Week 33

229 - 1

Ask him directly.
Demandu lin rekte.

229 - 2

I resemble my mother.
Mi similas al mia patrino.

229 - 3

Happy holidays!
Feliĉajn feriojn!

229 - 4

I am sorry to hear that.
Mi bedaŭras aŭdi tion.

229 - 5

This pipe is clogged.
Tiu ĉi tubo estas ŝtopiĝinta.

229 - 6

The baby is smiling.
La bebo ridetas.

229 - 7

She's very pretty.
Ŝi estas tre bela.

Day 229

Week 33

230 - 1

It's stifling hot.
Estas varmege sufoke.

230 - 2

Best regards.
Plej amike.

230 - 3

I am friendly person.
Mi estas amika homo.

230 - 4

It is not your fault.
Ne estas via kulpo.

230 - 5

What is the first step?
Kio estas la unua paŝo?

230 - 6

What is your shoe size?
Kio estas via ŝuo grandeco?

230 - 7

I read the times.
Mi legis la times.

Day 230

Test 33

231 - 1

It's very hot today.

231 - 2

The sun is glaring.

231 - 3

His grades are not bad.

231 - 4

I have strong teeth.

231 - 5

I resemble my mother.

231 - 6

It's stifling hot.

231 - 7

I read the times.

Day 231

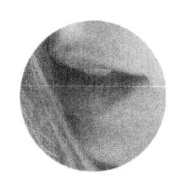

Week 34

232 - 1

Is there free wi-fi?
Ĉu estas senpaga wifi?

232 - 2

She closed her eyes.
Ŝi fermis la okulojn.

232 - 3

She has thick eyebrows.
Ŝi havas dikajn brovojn.

232 - 4

This is a danger zone.
Ĉi tio estas danĝera zono.

232 - 5

Just stay there.
Nur restu tie.

232 - 6

That was close.
Tio estis proksima.

232 - 7

Don't eat too much.
Ne manĝu tro multe.

Day 232

Week 34

233 - 1

He has feelings for her.
Li havas sentojn por ŝi.

233 - 2

He suddenly disappeared.
Li subite malaperis.

233 - 3

Please press the button.
Bonvolu premi la butonon.

233 - 4

What sport do you do?
Kian sporton vi faras?

233 - 5

It's twelve thirty.
Estas la dekdua kaj duono.

233 - 6

All the best, bye.
Ĉion bonan, adiaŭ.

233 - 7

This juice is too sweet.
Ĉi tiu suko estas tro dolĉa.

Day 233

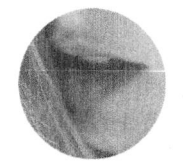

Week 34

234 - 1

I'm really sorry.
Mi vere bedaŭras.

234 - 2

The meeting is closed.
La kunveno estas fermita.

234 - 3

Hybrid vehicles only.
Hibridaj veturiloj nur.

234 - 4

Before you think, try.
Antaŭ ol vi pensas, provu.

234 - 5

Please sign here.
Bonvolu subskribi ĉi tie.

234 - 6

I remembered the past.
Mi rememoris la pasintecon.

234 - 7

How long will you wait?
Kiom longe vi atendos?

Day 234

Week 34

235 - 1

Nice to meet you too.
Ankaŭ plaĉas renkonti vin.

235 - 2

I feel chilly somehow.
Mi sentas min malvarma iel.

235 - 3

This apple's rotten.
Ĉi tiu pomo estas putra.

235 - 4

My head is spinning.
Mia kapo turniĝas.

235 - 5

There's a bird flying.
Tie flugas birdo.

235 - 6

I bought one book.
Mi aĉetis unu libron.

235 - 7

Our team lost the game.
Nia teamo perdis la ludon.

Day 235

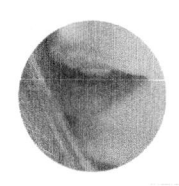

Week 34

236 - 1

Talk to you later.
Mi parolos al vi poste.

236 - 2

How do you know her?
Kiel vi konas ŝin?

236 - 3

He came on wednesday.
Li venis merkredon.

236 - 4

Stop fighting.
Ĉesu batali.

236 - 5

Why do you worry?
Kial vi maltrankviliĝas?

236 - 6

The ship sank.
La ŝipo subakviĝis.

236 - 7

He came by car.
Li venis per aŭtomobilo.

Day 236

Week 34

237 - 1

My kid wants some juice.
Mia infano volas iom da suko.

237 - 2

Is he learning english?
Ĉu li lernas la anglan?

237 - 3

Have you heard the news?
Ĉu vi aŭdis la novaĵon?

237 - 4

He has high ideals.
Li havas altajn idealojn.

237 - 5

Look up.
Rigardu supren.

237 - 6

Are you with me?
Ĉu vi estas kun mi?

237 - 7

Let's go to bed.
Ni enlitiĝos.

Day 237

Test 34

238 - 1

That was close.

238 - 2

It's twelve thirty.

238 - 3

Before you think, try.

238 - 4

This apple's rotten.

238 - 5

How do you know her?

34/52

238 - 6

My kid wants some juice.

238 - 7

Let's go to bed.

Day 238

Week 35

239 - 1

I don't play any sports.
Mi ne ludas sportojn.

239 - 2

My palms are sweaty.
Miaj manplatoj ŝvitas.

239 - 3

I changed the sheets.
Mi ŝanĝis la littukojn.

239 - 4

He made her very angry.
Li tre kolerigis ŝin.

239 - 5

I love cooking.
Mi amas kuiri.

239 - 6

You never listen to me.
Vi neniam aŭskultas min.

239 - 7

This way please.
Tiel bonvolu.

Day 239

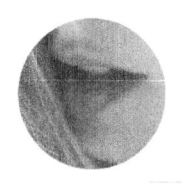

Week 35

240 - 1

Where are the shops?
Kie estas la butikoj?

240 - 2

A dash of pepper.
Guzeto da pipro.

240 - 3

It's been too long.
Pasis tro longa.

240 - 4

The brown bag is mine.
La bruna sako estas mia.

240 - 5

My son turned six.
Mia filo fariĝis sesjara.

35/52

240 - 6

I'm glad you like it.
Mi ĝojas, ke vi ŝatas ĝin.

240 - 7

This orange is sour.
Ĉi tiu oranĝo estas acida.

Day 240

Week 35

241 - 1

Good to see you.
Bone vidi vin.

241 - 2

I study philosophy.
Mi studas filozofion.

241 - 3

He's very intelligent.
Li estas tre inteligenta.

241 - 4

Enjoy your meal!
Ĝuu vian manĝon!

241 - 5

I'm called john.
Mi nomiĝas johano.

241 - 6

Judgment has been made.
Juĝo estas farita.

241 - 7

He should exercise more.
Li devus ekzerci pli.

Day 241

Week 35

242 - 1

That's not right.
Tio ne pravas.

242 - 2

Ask him not to go there.
Petu lin ne iri tien.

242 - 3

Work in progress.
Laboro en progreso.

242 - 4

What is your opinion?
Kion vi opinias?

242 - 5

Are you sure about it?
Ĉu vi certas pri tio?

242 - 6

It's cold in this room.
Estas malvarme en ĉi tiu ĉambro.

242 - 7

Is he at home?
Ĉu li estas hejme?

Day 242

Week 35

243 - 1

This sofa feels good.
Ĉi tiu sofo sentas bone.

243 - 2

He is my classmate.
Li estas mia samklasano.

243 - 3

Do you want a receipt?
Ĉu vi volas kvitancon?

243 - 4

I don't fell well.
Mi ne falis bone.

243 - 5

My nose is stuffed up.
Mia nazo estas plenigita.

243 - 6

Do you have a pen?
Ĉu vi havas plumon?

243 - 7

Who would like to read?
Kiu ŝatus legi?

Day 243

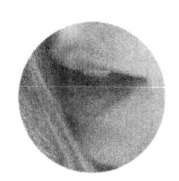

Week 35

244 - 1

Go and get dressed.
Iru kaj vestu vin.

244 - 2

This blanket is warm.
Ĉi tiu kovrilo estas varma.

244 - 3

What is your hobby?
Kio estas via ŝatokupo?

244 - 4

I banged on the door.
Mi frapis la pordon.

244 - 5

I don't watch much tv.
Mi ne multe spektas televidon.

244 - 6

Stop the car.
Haltu la aŭton.

244 - 7

Ice is a solid.
Glacio estas solida.

Day 244

Test 35

245 - 1

You never listen to me.

245 - 2

My son turned six.

245 - 3

Enjoy your meal!

245 - 4

Work in progress.

245 - 5

He is my classmate.

245 - 6

Go and get dressed.

245 - 7

Ice is a solid.

Day 245

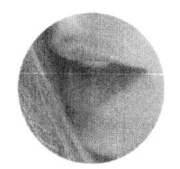

Week 36

246 - 1

He took a deep breath.
Li profunde enspiris.

246 - 2

It's very near.
Ĝi estas tre proksime.

246 - 3

This is a real diamond.
Ĉi tio estas vera diamanto.

246 - 4

Where do i have to sign?
Kie mi devas subskribi?

246 - 5

Happy valentine's day!
Feliĉan tagon de sankta valentín!

246 - 6

It's worth the price.
Ĝi valoras la prezon.

246 - 7

I wouldn't mind.
Mi ne ĝenus.

Day 246

Week 36

247 - 1

That was a great match!
Tio estis bonega matĉo!

247 - 2

Are you angry with me?
Ĉu vi koleras kontraŭ mi?

247 - 3

Read them aloud.
Legu ilin laŭtvoĉe.

247 - 4

She's a quick learner.
Ŝi estas rapida lernanto.

247 - 5

It's too loose.
Ĝi estas tro malfiksa.

247 - 6

The teacher guides us.
La instruisto gvidas nin.

247 - 7

What can i do for you?
Kion mi povas fari por vi?

Day 247

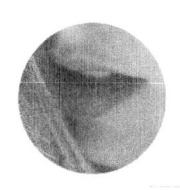

Week 36

248 - 1

Who do you go with?
Kun kiu vi iras?

248 - 2

It was my mistake.
Estis mia eraro.

248 - 3

Please hold on.
Bonvolu atendi.

248 - 4

Are you free tomorrow?
Ĉu vi estas libera morgaŭ?

248 - 5

I have a meeting today.
Mi havas kunvenon hodiaŭ.

248 - 6

Read it out loud.
Legu ĝin laŭte.

248 - 7

He never keeps secrets.
Li neniam konservas sekretojn.

Day 248

Week 36

249 - 1

Where is the hospital?
Kie estas la hospitalo?

249 - 2

His car is new.
Lia aŭto estas nova.

249 - 3

The view is incredible.
La vido estas nekredebla.

249 - 4

What is this?
Kio estas ĉi tio?

249 - 5

Can you hear me ok?
Ĉu vi povas aŭdi min bone?

249 - 6

No thanks, i'll pass.
Ne dankon, mi pasos.

249 - 7

One of my eyes is itchy.
Unu el miaj okuloj jukas.

Day 249

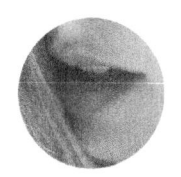

Week 36

250 - 1

Don't doubt yourself.
Ne dubu pri vi mem.

250 - 2

It's very kind of you.
Estas tre afabla de vi.

250 - 3

When is it?
Kiam ĝi estas?

250 - 4

Think nothing of it.
Pensu nenion pri ĝi.

250 - 5

Are you ready for this?
Ĉu vi pretas por ĉi tio?

250 - 6

I like strong tastes.
Mi ŝatas fortajn gustojn.

250 - 7

Where are you living?
Kie vi loĝas?

Day 250

Week 36

251 - 1

Let's meet this evening.
Ni renkontiĝu ĉi-vespere.

251 - 2

It's good to see you.
Estas bone vidi vin.

251 - 3

He's hurt his ankle.
Li vundis sian maleolon.

251 - 4

Did it rain there?
Ĉu tie pluvis?

251 - 5

Mince the garlic.
Piki la ajlon.

251 - 6

Gentle wet cleaning.
Milda malseka purigado.

251 - 7

I'm pleased to meet you.
Mi ĝojas renkonti vin.

Day 251

LEARN ESPERANTO IN 52 WEEKS

LEARN ESPERANTO IN 52 WEEKS WITH 7 SENTENCES A DAY

Test 36

252 - 1

It's worth the price.

252 - 2

It's too loose.

252 - 3

Are you free tomorrow?

252 - 4

The view is incredible.

252 - 5

It's very kind of you.

36/52

252 - 6

Let's meet this evening.

252 - 7

I'm pleased to meet you.

Day 252

Week 37

253 - 1

Is this organic?
Ĉu ĉi tio estas organika?

253 - 2

Call a fire brigade!
Voku fajrobrigadon!

253 - 3

They shook hands.
Ili manpremis.

253 - 4

It's not my fault.
Ne estas mia kulpo.

253 - 5

I need car insurance.
Mi bezonas aŭtoasekuron.

253 - 6

Please line up here.
Bonvolu viciĝi ĉi tie.

253 - 7

He is rich but stingy.
Li estas riĉa sed avara.

Day 253

Week 37

254 - 1

Is everyone injured?
Ĉu ĉiuj estas vunditaj?

254 - 2

Put on these pajamas.
Surmetu ĉi tiujn piĵamojn.

254 - 3

It's raining heavily.
Pluvas forte.

254 - 4

No cheating, please.
Neniu trompo, mi petas.

254 - 5

No, you cannot.
Ne, vi ne povas.

254 - 6

He is my colleague.
Li estas mia kolego.

254 - 7

He's still single.
Li ankoraŭ estas fraŭla.

Day 254

LEARN ESPERANTO IN 52 WEEKS

LEARN ESPERANTO IN 52 WEEKS WITH 7 SENTENCES A DAY

Week 37

255 - 1
We drank premium wine.
Ni trinkis altkvalitan vinon.

255 - 2
I feel nauseous.
Mi sentas naŭzon.

255 - 3
Could i speak to john?
Ĉu mi povus paroli kun johano?

255 - 4
Have a good time.
Amuziĝu.

255 - 5
I'd love to, thanks.
Mi ŝatus, dankon.

255 - 6
Save for a rainy day.
Konservu por pluva tago.

255 - 7
He turned the page.
Li turnis la paĝon.

Day 255

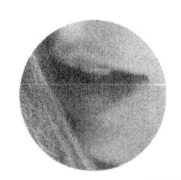

Week 37

256 - 1

He is a dentist.
Li estas dentisto.

256 - 2

A leaf fluttered down.
Folio flutis malsupren.

256 - 3

I was busy this evening.
Mi estis okupata ĉi-vespere.

256 - 4

Please give me that one.
Bonvolu doni al mi tiun.

256 - 5

Is there a bank here?
Ĉu estas banko ĉi tie?

256 - 6

I have no time.
Mi ne havas tempon.

256 - 7

My room is rectangular.
Mia ĉambro estas rektangula.

Day 256

Week 37

257 - 1

Let's begin.
Ni komencu.

257 - 2

I work under pressure.
Mi laboras sub premo.

257 - 3

I saw his album.
Mi vidis lian albumon.

257 - 4

I dyed my hair red.
Mi ruĝe tinkturigis miajn harojn.

257 - 5

Leave me alone.
Lasu min sola.

257 - 6

Stop chattering.
Ĉesu babili.

257 - 7

I admired his patience.
Mi admiris lian paciencon.

Day 257

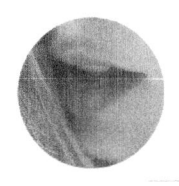

Week 37

258 - 1

We played a video game.
Ni ludis videoludon.

258 - 2

There's a sample here.
Estas specimeno ĉi tie.

258 - 3

My grandfather got sick.
Mia avo malsaniĝis.

258 - 4

He lives around here.
Li loĝas ĉi tie.

258 - 5

The flu spread rapidly.
La gripo disvastiĝis rapide.

258 - 6

Practice first aid.
Praktiku unuan helpon.

258 - 7

Better luck next time.
Pli bona sorto venontfoje.

Day 258

Test 37

259 - 1

Please line up here.

259 - 2

No, you cannot.

259 - 3

Have a good time.

259 - 4

I was busy this evening.

259 - 5

I work under pressure.

259 - 6

We played a video game.

259 - 7

Better luck next time.

Day 259

Week 38

260 - 1

It's windy.
Estas venta.

260 - 2

How's it going?
Kiel vi fartas?

260 - 3

He's not arrogant.
Li ne estas aroganta.

260 - 4

Is she writing a letter?
Ĉu ŝi skribas leteron?

260 - 5

I need a green blouse.
Mi bezonas verdan bluzon.

260 - 6

It doesn't matter to me.
Ne gravas al mi.

260 - 7

Do some yoga.
Faru jogon.

Day 260

Week 38

261 - 1

Turn left.
Turnu maldekstren.

261 - 2

Do not move the victim.
Ne movu la viktimon.

261 - 3

That's too bad.
Domaĝe.

261 - 4

Welcome to japan.
Bonvenon al japanio.

261 - 5

How are your grades?
Kiel estas viaj notoj?

261 - 6

Please sit there.
Bonvolu sidi tie.

261 - 7

I watered the plant.
Mi akvumis la planton.

Day 261

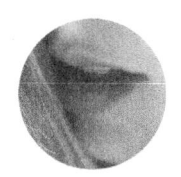

Week 38

262 - 1

I am a housewife.
Mi estas dommastrino.

262 - 2

We've run out of time.
Ni mankis tempo.

262 - 3

That's great.
Tio estas bonega.

262 - 4

She's tall.
Ŝi estas alta.

262 - 5

My boss is stubborn.
Mia estro estas obstina.

262 - 6

Why should i care?
Kial mi zorgu?

262 - 7

I like wooden houses.
Mi ŝatas lignajn domojn.

Day 262

Week 38

263 - 1

You look very handsome.
Vi aspektas tre bela.

263 - 2

I like wine.
Mi ŝatas vinon.

263 - 3

This is my teacher.
Ĉi tiu estas mia instruisto.

263 - 4

I just love to travel.
Mi nur amas vojaĝi.

263 - 5

He's very popular.
Li estas tre populara.

263 - 6

I beg your pardon.
Pardonu min.

263 - 7

Have you been lifting?
Ĉu vi levis?

Day 263

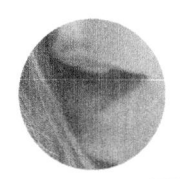

Week 38

264 - 1

I don't agree with you.
Mi ne konsentas kun vi.

264 - 2

I feel giddy.
Mi sentas kapturnon.

264 - 3

Don't do it again.
Ne faru ĝin denove.

264 - 4

Do you have any quirks?
Ĉu vi havas strangaĵojn?

264 - 5

We are hungry.
Ni malsatas.

264 - 6

He's a wonderful man.
Li estas mirinda viro.

264 - 7

Did you return the book?
Ĉu vi resendis la libron?

Day 264

Week 38

265 - 1

I'm fine, thank you.
Mi fartas bone, dankon.

265 - 2

Remember the date.
Memoru la daton.

265 - 3

Kiss me, my darling.
Kisu min, mia karulo.

265 - 4

Don't make noise.
Ne faru bruon.

265 - 5

Keep cool.
Konservu malvarmeta.

265 - 6

Does he act well?
Ĉu li bone agas?

265 - 7

Did you have breakfast?
Ĉu vi matenmanĝis?

Day 265

LEARN ESPERANTO IN 52 WEEKS

LEARN ESPERANTO IN 52 WEEKS WITH 7 SENTENCES A DAY

Test 38

266 - 1

It doesn't matter to me.

266 - 2

How are your grades?

266 - 3

She's tall.

266 - 4

This is my teacher.

266 - 5

I feel giddy.

266 - 6

I'm fine, thank you.

38/52

266 - 7

Did you have breakfast?

Day 266

LEARN ESPERANTO IN 52 WEEKS

LEARN ESPERANTO IN 52 WEEKS WITH 7 SENTENCES A DAY

Week 39

267 - 1

He watches movies a lot.
Li multe spektas filmojn.

267 - 2

I was glad to meet him.
Mi ĝojis renkonti lin.

267 - 3

Hi. i'm cindy.
Saluton. mi estas cindy.

267 - 4

I hate to tell you but.
Mi malamas diri al vi sed.

267 - 5

It is very far.
Estas tre malproksime.

267 - 6

Mind your tongue.
Atentu vian langon.

267 - 7

It was nothing really.
Estis nenio vere.

Day 267

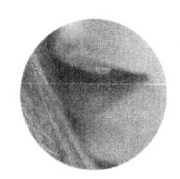

Week 39

268 - 1

Why are you late?
Kial vi malfruas?

268 - 2

Why are you asking me?
Kial vi demandas min?

268 - 3

Where's the post office?
Kie estas la poŝtoficejo?

268 - 4

What brings you here?
Kio venigas vin ĉi tien?

268 - 5

I took the first train.
Mi prenis la unuan trajnon.

268 - 6

His room is very dirty.
Lia ĉambro estas tre malpura.

268 - 7

The dog licked my face.
La hundo lekis mian vizaĝon.

Day 268

Week 39

269 - 1

He lost consciousness.
Li perdis konscion.

269 - 2

I hate the dentist.
Mi malamas la dentiston.

269 - 3

Let's check your papers.
Ni kontrolu viajn paperojn.

269 - 4

Which is the sauce?
Kiu estas la saŭco?

269 - 5

Can you forgive me?
Ĉu vi povas pardoni min?

269 - 6

She uses a wheelchair.
Ŝi uzas rulseĝon.

269 - 7

You look pale.
Vi aspektas pala.

Day 269

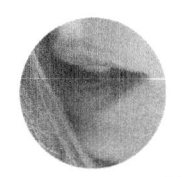

Week 39

270 - 1

I return home at 6.30.
Mi revenas hejmen je la 6.30.

270 - 2

Don't lose your temper.
Ne perdu vian humoron.

270 - 3

Good evening.
Bonan vesperon.

270 - 4

What's up?
Kio okazas?

270 - 5

He doesn't smoke.
Li ne fumas.

270 - 6

I won't go if it rains.
Mi ne iros se pluvos.

270 - 7

My wife is from london.
Mia edzino estas el londono.

Day 270

Week 39

271 - 1
Let's meet on monday.
Ni renkontiĝos lunde.

271 - 2
And i am good at it.
Kaj mi estas bona pri ĝi.

271 - 3
Is she calling you?
Ĉu ŝi vokas vin?

271 - 4
She's an office worker.
Ŝi estas oficejisto.

271 - 5
Time passes quickly.
La tempo pasas rapide.

271 - 6
He was overtaking.
Li preterpasis.

271 - 7
It's cold.
Malvarmas.

Day 271

Week 39

272 - 1

She's good at makeup.
Ŝi lertas pri ŝminko.

272 - 2

I added my own thought.
Mi aldonis mian propran penson.

272 - 3

I belong to oxford.
Mi apartenas al oksfordo.

272 - 4

A table for two?
Ĉu tablo por du?

272 - 5

Lock the door.
Ŝlosu la pordon.

272 - 6

Where does he work?
Kie li laboras?

272 - 7

He doesn't have time.
Li ne havas tempon.

Day 272

Test 39

273 - 1

Mind your tongue.

273 - 2

I took the first train.

273 - 3

Which is the sauce?

273 - 4

Good evening.

273 - 5

And i am good at it.

273 - 6

She's good at makeup.

273 - 7

He doesn't have time.

Day 273

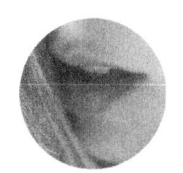

Week 40

274 - 1

He's still young.
Li estas ankoraŭ juna.

274 - 2

Do not cross.
Ne transiru.

274 - 3

Who told you?
Kiu diris al vi?

274 - 4

The floor is wet.
La planko estas malseka.

274 - 5

How's your day going?
Kiel iras via tago?

274 - 6

This work is hard.
Ĉi tiu laboro estas malfacila.

274 - 7

She's very honest.
Ŝi estas tre honesta.

Day 274

Week 40

275 - 1

Can i see the menu?
Ĉu mi povas vidi la menuon?

275 - 2

Where does he live?
Kie li loĝas?

275 - 3

He's a careful person.
Li estas singarda homo.

275 - 4

My card has been stolen.
Mia karto estas ŝtelita.

275 - 5

I don't know for sure.
Mi ne scias certe.

275 - 6

I met her in the town.
Mi renkontis ŝin en la urbo.

275 - 7

I've been tired today.
Mi estas laca hodiaŭ.

Day 275

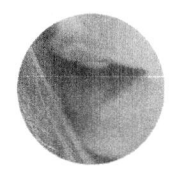

Week 40

276 - 1
I'll go.
Mi iros.

276 - 2
In my opinion.
Miaopinie.

276 - 3
Are you following me?
Ĉu vi sekvas min?

276 - 4
Does the bomb blast?
Ĉu la bombo eksplodas?

276 - 5
That girl is trendy.
Tiu knabino estas laŭmoda.

276 - 6
There are seven bananas.
Estas sep bananoj.

276 - 7
When do you return home?
Kiam vi revenas hejmen?

Day 276

Week 40

277 - 1

She had surgery.
Ŝi havis operacion.

277 - 2

Please include me.
Bonvolu inkluzivi min.

277 - 3

Open wide, please.
Larĝe malfermu, mi petas.

277 - 4

What's the time?
Kiom estas la horo?

277 - 5

This is confidential.
Ĉi tio estas konfidenca.

277 - 6

The water has boiled.
La akvo bolis.

277 - 7

It's nice to meet you.
Estas agrable renkonti vin.

Day 277

Week 40

278 - 1

I'm angry about.
Mi koleras pri.

278 - 2

It's a good deal.
Estas bona interkonsento.

278 - 3

A sheet of pastry.
Folio de kukaĵo.

278 - 4

She is my grandmother.
Ŝi estas mia avino.

278 - 5

No blowing of horns.
Neniu blovado de kornoj.

278 - 6

He's a serious student.
Li estas serioza studento.

278 - 7

Her cheeks are all red.
Ŝiaj vangoj estas ĉiuj ruĝaj.

Day 278

Week 40

279 - 1

Nice to meet you.
Mi ĝojas renkonti vin.

279 - 2

My bike got a flat tire.
Mia biciklo ricevis platpneŭon.

279 - 3

A person is missing.
Mankas homo.

279 - 4

She likes tall men.
Ŝi ŝatas altajn virojn.

279 - 5

That is okay.
Tio estas en ordo.

279 - 6

Is it serious?
Ĉu serioze?

279 - 7

I don't have some cash.
Mi ne havas monon.

Day 279

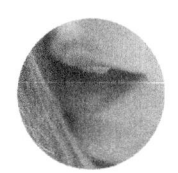

Test 40

280 - 1

This work is hard.

280 - 2

I don't know for sure.

280 - 3

Does the bomb blast?

280 - 4

Open wide, please.

280 - 5

It's a good deal.

280 - 6

Nice to meet you.

280 - 7

I don't have some cash.

Day 280

Week 41

281 - 1

Is this show good?
Ĉu ĉi tiu spektaklo estas bona?

281 - 2

Do the home work.
Faru la hejman laboron.

281 - 3

Which do you like best?
Kiun vi plej ŝatas?

281 - 4

I need life insurance.
Mi bezonas vivasekuron.

281 - 5

I'll go right away.
Mi tuj iros.

281 - 6

I am really cold.
Mi estas vere malvarma.

281 - 7

Don't rush me.
Ne rapidu min.

Day 281

Week 41

282 - 1

Do not smoke.
Ne fumu.

282 - 2

Have a walk.
Promenu.

282 - 3

Safety comes first.
Sekureco venas unue.

282 - 4

It is as you say.
Estas kiel vi diras.

282 - 5

Can i borrow a pen?
Ĉu mi povas prunti plumon?

282 - 6

He was nervous.
Li estis nervoza.

282 - 7

This food is tasteless.
Ĉi tiu manĝaĵo estas sengusta.

Day 282

Week 41

283 - 1

It's yummy.
Ĝi estas bongusta.

283 - 2

The man stole her bag.
La viro ŝtelis ŝian sakon.

283 - 3

It's your decision.
Estas via decido.

283 - 4

I like thin pillows.
Mi ŝatas maldikajn kusenojn.

283 - 5

Many happy returns.
Multaj feliĉaj revenoj.

283 - 6

Raise your hands.
Levu viajn manojn.

283 - 7

Are you being served?
Ĉu vi estas servata?

Day 283

Week 41

284 - 1

My boss gave me his car.
Mia estro donis al mi sian aŭton.

284 - 2

I have a sore throat.
Mi havas gorĝdoloron.

284 - 3

Thank you so much!
Multan dankon!

284 - 4

Who are your bankers?
Kiuj estas viaj bankistoj?

284 - 5

Are you aware of that?
Ĉu vi konscias pri tio?

284 - 6

You must not.
Vi ne devas.

284 - 7

Do me a favor.
Faru al mi favoron.

Day 284

Week 41

285 - 1

I didn't wake up early.
Mi ne vekiĝis frue.

285 - 2

What time can we meet?
Je kioma horo ni povas renkontiĝi?

285 - 3

I'll be glad to do so.
Mi ĝojos fari tion.

285 - 4

It's hot.
Estas varme.

285 - 5

Do you think it is true?
Ĉu vi pensas, ke ĝi estas vera?

285 - 6

Good afternoon, mrs.
Bonan posttagmezon, s-ino.

285 - 7

A new year has started.
Nova jaro komenciĝis.

Day 285

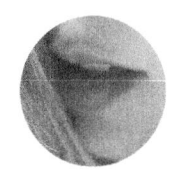

Week 41

286 - 1

The answer is wrong.
La respondo estas malĝusta.

286 - 2

He joined our team.
Li aliĝis al nia teamo.

286 - 3

Do like your job?
Ĉu vi ŝatas vian laboron?

286 - 4

I go to a gym.
Mi iras al gimnazio.

286 - 5

How is your husband?
Kiel fartas via edzo?

286 - 6

I get up at 6.30.
Mi ellitiĝas je la 6.30.

286 - 7

He has big arms.
Li havas grandajn brakojn.

Day 286

Test 41

287 - 1

I am really cold.

287 - 2

Can i borrow a pen?

287 - 3

I like thin pillows.

287 - 4

Thank you so much!

287 - 5

What time can we meet?

287 - 6

The answer is wrong.

287 - 7

He has big arms.

Day 287

Week 42

288 - 1

That's a nuisance.
Tio estas ĝeno.

288 - 2

No entry for bicycles.
Neniu eniro por bicikloj.

288 - 3

May i take a message?
Ĉu mi rajtas preni mesaĝon?

288 - 4

I like your haircut.
Mi ŝatas vian hartondon.

288 - 5

I hate carrots.
Mi malamas karotojn.

288 - 6

Where do i come from?
De kie mi venas?

288 - 7

I love lobsters.
Mi amas omarojn.

Day 288

Week 42

289 - 1

Do not lean.
Ne kliniĝu.

289 - 2

Nice of you to make it.
Bone de vi fari ĝin.

289 - 3

No parking.
Neniu parkado.

289 - 4

I'm studying japanese.
Mi studas la japanan.

289 - 5

I've got to go now.
Mi devas iri nun.

289 - 6

Have a drink.
Trinku.

289 - 7

Wait for sometime.
Atendu iam.

Day 289

Week 42

290 - 1

That shirt looks cheap.
Tiu ĉemizo aspektas malmultekosta.

290 - 2

I like french food.
Mi ŝatas francan manĝaĵon.

290 - 3

Please be seated.
Bonvolu sidiĝi.

290 - 4

Does he have a pulse?
Ĉu li havas pulson?

290 - 5

I missed the bus.
Mi maltrafis la buson.

290 - 6

I'm thirty.
Mi estas tridekjara.

290 - 7

You are not allowed to.
Vi ne rajtas.

Day 290

Week 42

291 - 1

I have mouth sores.
Mi havas buŝulojn.

291 - 2

I'm impressed.
Mi estas impresita.

291 - 3

She injured her arm.
Ŝi vundis sian brakon.

291 - 4

My name is john.
Mia nomo estas johano.

291 - 5

I am a social worker.
Mi estas socia laboristo.

291 - 6

How old is your son?
Kiom da jaroj havas via filo?

291 - 7

The line is busy.
La linio estas okupata.

Day 291

Week 42

292 - 1

I bought a leather belt.
Mi aĉetis ledan zonon.

292 - 2

Do you think so?
Ĉu vi pensas tiel?

292 - 3

Get out of my sight.
Foriru de mia vido.

292 - 4

He was sent to england.
Li estis sendita al anglio.

292 - 5

Do you hate him?
Ĉu vi malamas lin?

292 - 6

Please, come in.
Bonvolu enveni.

292 - 7

What a beautiful house!
Kia bela domo!

Day 292

Week 42

293 - 1

I tend to think that.
Mi emas pensi tion.

293 - 2

I inhaled dust.
Mi enspiris polvon.

293 - 3

Brilliant idea!
Brila ideo!

293 - 4

Did you enjoy your meal?
Ĉu vi ĝuis vian manĝon?

293 - 5

I have some books.
Mi havas kelkajn librojn.

293 - 6

I bought a new computer.
Mi aĉetis novan komputilon.

293 - 7

What is he?
Kio estas li?

Day 293

LEARN ESPERANTO IN 52 WEEKS

LEARN ESPERANTO IN 52 WEEKS WITH 7 SENTENCES A DAY

Test 42

294 - 1

Where do i come from?

294 - 2

I've got to go now.

294 - 3

Does he have a pulse?

294 - 4

She injured her arm.

294 - 5

Do you think so?

294 - 6

I tend to think that.

294 - 7

What is he?

Day 294

Week 43

295 - 1

I can't move.
Mi ne povas movi.

295 - 2

The child woke up.
La infano vekiĝis.

295 - 3

I prefer rice to bread.
Mi preferas rizon al pano.

295 - 4

May i take your order?
Ĉu mi rajtas preni vian mendon?

295 - 5

I took on a new job.
Mi prenis novan laboron.

295 - 6

It's 16th june.
Estas la 16-a de junio.

295 - 7

By all means.
Por ĉiuj rimedoj.

Day 295

LEARN ESPERANTO IN 52 WEEKS
LEARN ESPERANTO IN 52 WEEKS WITH 7 SENTENCES A DAY

Week 43

296 - 1

I'm absolutely sure.
Mi estas tute certa.

296 - 2

May i know your name?
Ĉu mi rajtas scii vian nomon?

296 - 3

I really like you.
Mi vere ŝatas vin.

296 - 4

It's too tight for me.
Ĝi estas tro streĉa por mi.

296 - 5

I am so into you.
Mi tiom ŝatas vin.

296 - 6

It's raining.
Pluvas.

296 - 7

She hasn't noticed me.
Ŝi ne rimarkis min.

Day 296

Week 43

297 - 1

Where are you now?
Kie vi estas nun?

297 - 2

Who is this man?
Kiu estas ĉi tiu viro?

297 - 3

What's going on?
Kio okazas?

297 - 4

This bag is heavy.
Ĉi tiu sako estas peza.

297 - 5

This car is very fast.
Ĉi tiu aŭto estas tre rapida.

297 - 6

I didn't order that.
Mi ne mendis tion.

297 - 7

Please call me at home.
Bonvolu telefoni al mi hejme.

Day 297

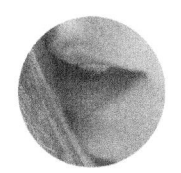

Week 43

298 - 1

Mind the steps.
Atentu la paŝojn.

298 - 2

Best wishes.
Bondezirojn.

298 - 3

My throat is a bit dry.
Mia gorĝo estas iom seka.

298 - 4

I jog every day.
Mi trotadas ĉiutage.

298 - 5

Her skin is very white.
Ŝia haŭto estas tre blanka.

298 - 6

Is she cutting a tree?
Ĉu ŝi trancas arbon?

298 - 7

My wallet is empty.
Mia monujo estas malplena.

Day 298

Week 43

299 - 1

Anything else?
Ĉu io alia?

299 - 2

The test was very easy.
La testo estis tre facila.

299 - 3

I was moved to tears.
Mi estis kortuŝita ĝis larmoj.

299 - 4

He's full of energy.
Li estas plena de energio.

299 - 5

He became a doctor.
Li fariĝis kuracisto.

299 - 6

I like watching t.v.
Mi ŝatas spekti t.v.

43/52

299 - 7

Can you drive a truck?
Ĉu vi povas stiri kamionon?

Day 299

Week 43

300 - 1

I was the one to blame.
Mi estis la kulpa.

300 - 2

Which one of these?
Kiu el ĉi tiuj?

300 - 3

Can you hear me?
Ĉu vi povas aŭdi min?

300 - 4

My son broke my glasses.
Mia filo rompis miajn okulvitrojn.

300 - 5

How did you reach there?
Kiel vi atingis tie?

300 - 6

I was stuck in traffic.
Mi estis blokita en trafiko.

300 - 7

Please hold the door.
Bonvolu teni la pordon.

Day 300

Test 43

301 - 1

It's 16th june.

301 - 2

I am so into you.

301 - 3

This bag is heavy.

301 - 4

My throat is a bit dry.

301 - 5

The test was very easy.

301 - 6

I was the one to blame.

301 - 7

Please hold the door.

Day 301

Week 44

302 - 1

I peeled a carrot.
Mi senŝeligis karoton.

302 - 2

This ball bounces well.
Ĉi tiu pilko bone resaltas.

302 - 3

How much should i pay?
Kiom mi pagu?

302 - 4

Why did you beat him?
Kial vi batis lin?

302 - 5

Where do they live?
Kie ili loĝas?

302 - 6

I am ready.
Mi pretas.

302 - 7

It's a pleasant morning.
Estas agrabla mateno.

Day 302

Week 44

303 - 1

I think you're wrong.
Mi pensas, ke vi eraras.

303 - 2

My hobby is reading.
Mia ŝatokupo estas legi.

303 - 3

I'm painting the wall.
Mi pentras la muron.

303 - 4

The pool is packed.
La naĝejo estas plenplena.

303 - 5

He's a very kind person.
Li estas tre afabla homo.

303 - 6

Who's speaking?
Kiu parolas?

303 - 7

A sack of rice.
Sako da rizo.

Day 303

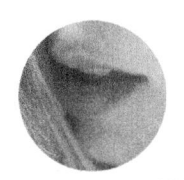

Week 44

304 - 1

Get enough sleep.
Dormu sufiĉe.

304 - 2

The bathroom is there.
La banĉambro estas tie.

304 - 3

Can you speak english?
Ĉu vi povas paroli la anglan?

304 - 4

Do you have a stool?
Ĉu vi havas tabureton?

304 - 5

Oh, my god. really?
Ho, mia dio. ĉu vere?

304 - 6

He has long legs.
Li havas longajn krurojn.

304 - 7

My shoulders are stiff.
Miaj ŝultroj estas rigidaj.

Day 304

Week 44

305 - 1

Did he say anything?
Ĉu li diris ion?

305 - 2

What's wrong?
Kio estas malbona?

305 - 3

Anything to convey?
Ion por transdoni?

305 - 4

There's one problem.
Estas unu problemo.

305 - 5

I feel powerful.
Mi sentas min potenca.

305 - 6

It's your mistake.
Estas via eraro.

305 - 7

Have a safe flight!
Havu sekuran flugon!

Day 305

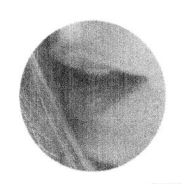

Week 44

306 - 1

He's a taxi driver.
Li estas taksiisto.

306 - 2

Don't threaten me.
Ne minacu min.

306 - 3

She has fat legs.
Ŝi havas grasajn krurojn.

306 - 4

Who am i talking to?
Kun kiu mi parolas?

306 - 5

Hold the line, please.
Tenu la linion, mi petas.

306 - 6

I got a promotion today.
Mi ricevis reklamon hodiaŭ.

306 - 7

I don't like to wait.
Mi ne ŝatas atendi.

Day 306

Week 44

307 - 1

She glared at me.
Ŝi rigardegis min.

307 - 2

I feel lazy to get up.
Mi sentas min mallaborema leviĝi.

307 - 3

Let's order first.
Ni unue mendu.

307 - 4

She wore a purple dress.
Ŝi portis purpuran robon.

307 - 5

How is everybody?
Kiel ĉiuj fartas?

307 - 6

It's too short.
Ĝi estas tro mallonga.

307 - 7

Here's the menu.
Jen la menuo.

Day 307

Test 44

308 - 1

I am ready.

308 - 2

He's a very kind person.

308 - 3

Do you have a stool?

308 - 4

Anything to convey?

308 - 5

Don't threaten me.

308 - 6

She glared at me.

308 - 7

Here's the menu.

Day 308

Week 45

309 - 1

She has lots of clothes.
Ŝi havas multajn vestaĵojn.

309 - 2

He apologized at once.
Li tuj pardonpetis.

309 - 3

I have a bad cold.
Mi havas malbonan malvarmumon.

309 - 4

She has blue eyes.
Ŝi havas bluajn okulojn.

309 - 5

She's a quiet person.
Ŝi estas trankvila homo.

309 - 6

Start the engine.
Ekfunkciigu la motoron.

309 - 7

Poor you.
Kompatinda vi.

Day 309

Week 45

310 - 1

The train is crowded.
La trajno estas plenplena.

310 - 2

I can do it.
Mi povas fari tion.

310 - 3

I need a lot of money.
Mi bezonas multe da mono.

310 - 4

Ice floats on water.
Glacio flosas sur akvo.

310 - 5

I'll go there by train.
Mi iros tien per trajno.

310 - 6

Are you john?
Ĉu vi estas johano?

310 - 7

How deep is the pool?
Kiom profunda estas la naĝejo?

Day 310

Week 45

311 - 1

Thanks so much.
Koran dankon.

311 - 2

How much is this?
Kiom ĉi tio kostas?

311 - 3

I received a threat.
Mi ricevis minacon.

311 - 4

We're classmates.
Ni estas samklasanoj.

311 - 5

I can help you.
Mi povas helpi vin.

311 - 6

James is my husband.
Jakobo estas mia edzo.

311 - 7

What do you want?
Kion vi volas?

Day 311

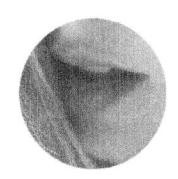

Week 45

312 - 1

Go ahead.
Antaŭeniri.

312 - 2

That's so sad.
Tio estas tiel malĝoja.

312 - 3

It is direct?
Ĉu estas rekta?

312 - 4

I apologize for.
Mi pardonpetas pro.

312 - 5

I like dogs a lot.
Mi tre ŝatas hundojn.

312 - 6

Turn right.
Turnu dekstren.

312 - 7

She has good manners.
Ŝi havas bonajn manierojn.

Day 312

Week 45

313 - 1

It was nobody's fault.
Nenies kulpo.

313 - 2

Let's pay separately.
Ni pagu aparte.

313 - 3

Your name please?
Via nomo mi petas?

313 - 4

I am sorry i'm late.
Mi bedaŭras, ke mi malfruas.

313 - 5

The road is closed.
La vojo estas fermita.

313 - 6

His story is boring.
Lia rakonto estas enuiga.

313 - 7

A leaf of lettuce.
Folio de laktuko.

Day 313

Week 45

314 - 1

Right of way changed.
Vojrajto ŝanĝiĝis.

314 - 2

He has a rich spirit.
Li havas riĉan spiriton.

314 - 3

I had a scary dream.
Mi havis timigan sonĝon.

314 - 4

It's very unlikely.
Estas tre neverŝajna.

314 - 5

It was a very sad movie.
Ĝi estis tre malĝoja filmo.

314 - 6

First day of school.
Unua tago de lernejo.

314 - 7

I don't get it.
Mi ne komprenas ĝin.

Day 314

Test 45

315 - 1

Start the engine.

315 - 2

I'll go there by train.

315 - 3

We're classmates.

315 - 4

It is direct?

315 - 5

Let's pay separately.

315 - 6

Right of way changed.

315 - 7

I don't get it.

Day 315

Week 46

316 - 1

I love my family.
Mi amas mian familion.

316 - 2

She talks a lot.
Ŝi multe parolas.

316 - 3

If only he were here!
Se nur li estus ĉi tie!

316 - 4

I like grapes.
Mi ŝatas vinberojn.

316 - 5

He is very sensitive.
Li estas tre sentema.

316 - 6

No classes tomorrow.
Neniuj klasoj morgaŭ.

316 - 7

Cool down.
Malvarmiĝi.

Day 316

Week 46

317 - 1

See you tomorrow.
Ĝis morgaŭ.

317 - 2

They speak french.
Ili parolas la francan.

317 - 3

She saved a sick dog.
Ŝi savis malsanan hundon.

317 - 4

I go by cycle.
Mi iras per ciklo.

317 - 5

Don't be afraid.
Ne timu.

317 - 6

You must be tired
Vi devas esti laca

317 - 7

I waited two days.
Mi atendis du tagojn.

Day 317

LEARN ESPERANTO IN 52 WEEKS

LEARN ESPERANTO IN 52 WEEKS WITH 7 SENTENCES A DAY

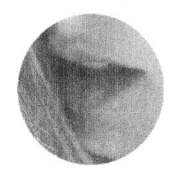

Week 46

318 - 1
Where's the bank?
Kie estas la banko?

318 - 2
I've got a sore throat.
Mi havas gorĝodoloron.

318 - 3
Please call this number.
Bonvolu voki ĉi tiun numeron.

318 - 4
Where is the station?
Kie estas la stacidomo?

318 - 5
Stop making excuses.
Ĉesu fari ekskuzojn.

318 - 6
Do not lie.
Ne mensogu.

318 - 7
This bra is too large.
Ĉi tiu mamzono estas tro granda.

46/52

Day 318

Week 46

319 - 1

Do as you like.
Faru kiel vi volas.

319 - 2

I live on my own.
Mi vivas memstare.

319 - 3

I need a new toothbrush.
Mi bezonas novan dentobroson.

319 - 4

This is a small town.
Ĉi tio estas urbeto.

319 - 5

He dared to face danger.
Li kuraĝis alfronti danĝeron.

319 - 6

The building collapsed.
La konstruaĵo kolapsis.

319 - 7

The deadline is near.
La limdato estas proksima.

Day 319

Week 46

320 - 1

How does it work?
Kiel ĝi funkcias?

320 - 2

Can i have one?
Ĉu mi povas havi unu?

320 - 3

She's feminine.
Ŝi estas ina.

320 - 4

I sat down on the bench.
Mi sidiĝis sur la benkon.

320 - 5

Yes, i've got one.
Jes, mi havas unu.

320 - 6

I go by scooter.
Mi iras per skotero.

320 - 7

What's the problem?
Kio estas la problemo?

Day 320

Week 46

321 - 1

I love my father.
Mi amas mian patron.

321 - 2

His face was all red.
Lia vizaĝo estis tute ruĝa.

321 - 3

I think so, too.
Ankaŭ mi pensas tiel.

321 - 4

No, not at all.
Ne, tute ne.

321 - 5

What a pity.
Kia domaĝo.

321 - 6

Don't ask me anything.
Ne demandu al mi ion ajn.

321 - 7

My passport is missing.
Mia pasporto mankas.

Day 321

Test 46

322 - 1

No classes tomorrow.

322 - 2

Don't be afraid.

322 - 3

Where is the station?

322 - 4

I need a new toothbrush.

322 - 5

Can i have one?

322 - 6

I love my father.

322 - 7

My passport is missing.

Day 322

Week 47

323 - 1

You can try it.
Vi povas provi ĝin.

323 - 2

The train door opened.
La trajnopordo malfermiĝis.

323 - 3

Send him out.
Sendu lin eksteren.

323 - 4

I am rather shy.
Mi estas iom timema.

323 - 5

I work in a factory.
Mi laboras en fabriko.

323 - 6

The sweater has shrunk.
La svetero ŝrumpis.

323 - 7

I got a perfect score.
Mi ricevis perfektan poentaron.

Day 323

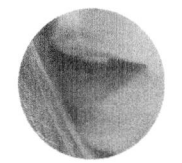

Week 47

324 - 1

We are six persons.
Ni estas ses personoj.

324 - 2

She was born in paris.
Ŝi naskiĝis en parizo.

324 - 3

My teeth are strong.
Miaj dentoj estas fortaj.

324 - 4

He won the election.
Li venkis en la elekto.

324 - 5

I did my best.
Mi faris mian plejeblon.

324 - 6

Stop playing pranks.
Ĉesu ludi petolojn.

324 - 7

It will rain tomorrow.
Pluvos morgaŭ.

Day 324

Week 47

325 - 1

Is he binding a book?
Ĉu li bindigas libron?

325 - 2

I will call you later.
Mi vokos vin poste.

325 - 3

When you've finished,
Kiam vi finos,

325 - 4

I am john.
Mi estas johano.

325 - 5

Where's the station?
Kie estas la stacidomo?

325 - 6

No one knows that story.
Neniu konas tiun historion.

325 - 7

I will buy it.
Mi aĉetos ĝin.

Day 325

Week 47

326 - 1

Meet them in person.
Renkontu ilin persone.

326 - 2

He's studying now.
Li nun studas.

326 - 3

Take this road.
Prenu ĉi tiun vojon.

326 - 4

That's all for today.
Tio estas ĉio por hodiaŭ.

326 - 5

I do not like you.
Mi ne ŝatas vin.

326 - 6

Where is his residence?
Kie estas lia loĝejo?

326 - 7

Milk was sold out.
Lakto estis elĉerpita.

Day 326

Week 47

327 - 1

Is john in?
Ĉu johano estas en?

327 - 2

I feel happy.
Mi sentas min feliĉa.

327 - 3

All right.
Bone.

327 - 4

I agree.
Mi konsentas.

327 - 5

Is your wife employed?
Ĉu via edzino estas dungita?

327 - 6

He felt miserable.
Li sentis sin mizera.

327 - 7

That's an extreme idea.
Tio estas ekstrema ideo.

Day 327

Week 47

328 - 1

This one is cheaper.
Ĉi tiu estas pli malmultekosta.

328 - 2

Please come.
Bonvolu veni.

328 - 3

Where did he come?
Kien li venis?

328 - 4

Just a moment please.
Nur momenton bonvolu.

328 - 5

Let's share more ideas.
Ni dividu pli da ideoj.

328 - 6

He is my father.
Li estas mia patro.

328 - 7

Pedestrian bridge.
Piedira ponto.

Day 328

Test 47

329 - 1

The sweater has shrunk.

329 - 2

I did my best.

329 - 3

I am john.

329 - 4

Take this road.

329 - 5

I feel happy.

329 - 6

This one is cheaper.

329 - 7

Pedestrian bridge.

Day 329

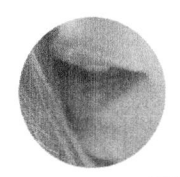

Week 48

330 - 1

How do i?
Kiel mi?

330 - 2

We all saw him off.
Ni ĉiuj vidis lin for.

330 - 3

We sang loudly.
Ni kantis laŭte.

330 - 4

It's 6 a.m now.
Nun estas la 6-a horo.

330 - 5

I prefer reading books.
Mi preferas legi librojn.

330 - 6

I have my own doubts.
Mi havas miajn proprajn dubojn.

330 - 7

My pleasure.
Mia plezuro.

Day 330

Week 48

331 - 1

Don't lose your receipt!
Ne perdu vian kvitancon!

331 - 2

My watch is stopped.
Mia horloĝo estas haltigita.

331 - 3

Can i open the windows?
Ĉu mi povas malfermi la fenestrojn?

331 - 4

All are fine.
Ĉiuj estas bone.

331 - 5

I have college today.
Mi havas kolegion hodiaŭ.

331 - 6

I arrived home safely.
Mi alvenis hejmen sekure.

331 - 7

How did they escape?
Kiel ili eskapis?

Day 331

Week 48

332 - 1

What is your score?
Kio estas via poentaro?

332 - 2

This book is difficult.
Ĉi tiu libro estas malfacila.

332 - 3

Is she going to delhi?
Ĉu ŝi iras al delhio?

332 - 4

Could i have a receipt?
Ĉu mi povus havi kvitancon?

332 - 5

Have you ever had a pet?
Ĉu vi iam havis dorlotbeston?

332 - 6

We are open all day.
Ni estas malfermitaj la tutan tagon.

332 - 7

Where's the library?
Kie estas la biblioteko?

Day 332

Week 48

333 - 1

Can you help me?
Ĉu vi povas helpi min?

333 - 2

I go by bus.
Mi iras per buso.

333 - 3

Will they come here?
Ĉu ili venos ĉi tien?

333 - 4

These shoes fit me.
Ĉi tiuj ŝuoj taŭgas por mi.

333 - 5

He is frequently late.
Li ofte malfruas.

333 - 6

Where is the baker's?
Kie estas la bakisto?

333 - 7

Do you play any sports?
Ĉu vi ludas sportojn?

Day 333

Week 48

334 - 1

Have dinner.
Vespermanĝi.

334 - 2

The rain stopped.
La pluvo ĉesis.

334 - 3

No one knows the future.
Neniu konas la estontecon.

334 - 4

What size do you wear?
Kiun grandecon vi portas?

334 - 5

I bought a new table.
Mi aĉetis novan tablon.

334 - 6

It is quite tasty.
Ĝi estas sufiĉe bongusta.

334 - 7

What about you?
Kio pri vi?

Day 334

Week 48

335 - 1

Is everything alright?
Ĉu ĉio estas en ordo?

335 - 2

Bear in mind.
Memoru.

335 - 3

I'm from roma.
Mi estas el romao.

335 - 4

You are welcome.
Nedankinde.

335 - 5

Are you alright?
Ĉu vi bonfartas?

335 - 6

I'm very hungry.
Mi tre malsatas.

335 - 7

I am from paris.
Mi estas el parizo.

Day 335

Test 48

336 - 1

I have my own doubts.

336 - 2

I have college today.

336 - 3

Could i have a receipt?

336 - 4

Will they come here?

336 - 5

The rain stopped.

336 - 6

Is everything alright?

336 - 7

I am from paris.

48/52

Day 336

Week 49

337 - 1

I met her downtown.
Mi renkontis ŝin en la urbocentro.

337 - 2

I feel a little sad.
Mi sentas min iom malĝoja.

337 - 3

Incredible.
Nekredebla.

337 - 4

No homework for today.
Neniuj hejmtaskoj por hodiaŭ.

337 - 5

It's sunny.
Estas sune.

337 - 6

The last step is.
La lasta paŝo estas.

337 - 7

I got a full massage.
Mi ricevis plenan masaĝon.

Day 337

Week 49

338 - 1

Can i use the gym?
Ĉu mi povas uzi la gimnazion?

338 - 2

Eat a balanced diet.
Manĝu ekvilibran dieton.

338 - 3

Smoking area.
Areo de fumado.

338 - 4

I feel very depressed.
Mi sentas min tre deprimita.

338 - 5

I go to bed at 10.30.
Mi enlitiĝas je la 10.30.

338 - 6

He's sometimes late.
Li kelkfoje malfruas.

338 - 7

Are they your relatives?
Ĉu ili estas viaj parencoj?

Day 338

Week 49

339 - 1

I'm a little tired.
Mi estas iom laca.

339 - 2

That's too expensive.
Tio estas tro multekosta.

339 - 3

What do you think?
Kion vi pensas?

339 - 4

It is really disgusting.
Estas vere abomena.

339 - 5

I looked up at the sky.
Mi rigardis supren al la ĉielo.

339 - 6

Are you satisfied now?
Ĉu vi nun estas kontenta?

339 - 7

I'm grilling fish now.
Mi rostas fiŝojn nun.

Day 339

LEARN ESPERANTO IN 52 WEEKS

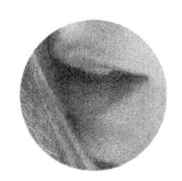

LEARN ESPERANTO IN 52 WEEKS WITH 7 SENTENCES A DAY

Week 49

340 - 1
Draw a big circle there.
Desegnu grandan cirklon tie.

340 - 2
Have a pizza.
Havu picon.

340 - 3
A coffee please.
Kafon mi petas.

340 - 4
He's just a drunkard.
Li estas nur drinkulo.

340 - 5
What time is my flight?
Je kioma horo estas mia flugo?

340 - 6
I'll join you.
Mi aliĝos al vi.

340 - 7
What did you do?
Kion vi faris?

Day 340

Week 49

341 - 1

Let's meet again.
Ni renkontu denove.

341 - 2

Ask him to call me.
Petu lin voki min.

341 - 3

The earth is round.
La tero estas ronda.

341 - 4

I want to gain weight.
Mi volas akiri pezon.

341 - 5

Does the water boil?
Ĉu la akvo bolas?

341 - 6

Stop here at red.
Haltu ĉi tie ĉe ruĝa.

341 - 7

The food smells good.
La manĝaĵo bone odoras.

Day 341

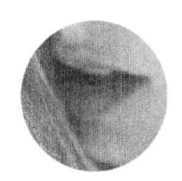

Week 49

342 - 1

Is the rumor true?
Ĉu la famo estas vera?

342 - 2

What are you doing?
Kion vi faras?

342 - 3

When did he come?
Kiam li venis?

342 - 4

Your number please.
Via numero bonvolu.

342 - 5

I broke my arm.
Mi rompis mian brakon.

342 - 6

I want to live abroad.
Mi volas vivi eksterlande.

342 - 7

Don't come near me.
Ne alproksimiĝu al mi.

Day 342

Test 49

343 - 1
The last step is.

343 - 2
I go to bed at 10.30.

343 - 3
It is really disgusting.

343 - 4
A coffee please.

343 - 5
Ask him to call me.

343 - 6
Is the rumor true?

343 - 7
Don't come near me.

Day 343

Week 50

344 - 1

Absolutely.
Absolute.

344 - 2

What was your best trip?
Kio estis via plej bona vojaĝo?

344 - 3

I am an engineer.
Mi estas inĝeniero.

344 - 4

That is 100% cotton.
Tio estas 100% kotono.

344 - 5

What street is this?
Kiu strato estas ĉi tiu?

344 - 6

What is my room number?
Kio estas mia ĉambronumero?

344 - 7

I like this show.
Mi ŝatas ĉi tiun spektaklon.

Day 344

Week 50

345 - 1

I love animals.
Mi amas bestojn.

345 - 2

I got drunk last night.
Mi ebriiĝis hieraŭ nokte.

345 - 3

Bye for now.
Ĝis nun.

345 - 4

Where is the bus stop?
Kie estas la bushaltejo?

345 - 5

There's nothing here.
Estas nenio ĉi tie.

345 - 6

Who knows the answer?
Kiu scias la respondon?

345 - 7

I am so sorry.
Mi tiom bedaŭras.

Day 345

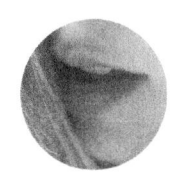

Week 50

346 - 1

Did you listen to me?
Ĉu vi aŭskultis min?

346 - 2

Please help yourself.
Bonvolu helpi vin.

346 - 3

I'm very sleepy today.
Mi estas tre dormema hodiaŭ.

346 - 4

Our cat had kittens.
Nia kato havis katidojn.

346 - 5

Why do you suspect me?
Kial vi suspektas min?

346 - 6

What time does it start?
Je kioma horo ĝi komenciĝas?

346 - 7

A pack of vitamins.
Pako da vitaminoj.

Day 346

Week 50

347 - 1

I didn't mean to.
Mi ne intencis.

347 - 2

Everyone has flaws.
Ĉiuj havas mankojn.

347 - 3

Today is a holiday.
Hodiaŭ estas ferio.

347 - 4

I couldn't agree more.
Mi ne povus pli konsenti.

347 - 5

Please check the tyres.
Bonvolu kontroli la pneŭojn.

347 - 6

Open your books.
Malfermu viajn librojn.

347 - 7

Please give me a minute.
Bonvolu doni al mi minuton.

Day 347

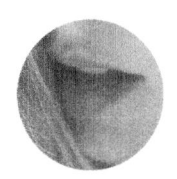

Week 50

348 - 1

I'm a student.
Mi estas studento.

348 - 2

Show your solutions.
Montru viajn solvojn.

348 - 3

He has six children.
Li havas ses infanojn.

348 - 4

The house is beautiful.
La domo estas bela.

348 - 5

Are you on facebook?
Ĉu vi estas en fejsbuko?

348 - 6

I love cats.
Mi amas katojn.

348 - 7

He's surely a hero.
Li certe estas heroo.

Day 348

Week 50

349 - 1

My sister is kind.
Mia fratino estas afabla.

349 - 2

Whom do you suspect?
Kiun vi suspektas?

349 - 3

Where's the bookshop?
Kie estas la librejo?

349 - 4

Please stop joking.
Bonvolu ĉesi ŝerci.

349 - 5

The traffic is clear.
La trafiko estas klara.

349 - 6

I hear a strange sound.
Mi aŭdas strangan sonon.

349 - 7

Do you sell swimsuits?
Ĉu vi vendas naĝkostumojn?

Day 349

Test 50

350 - 1
What is my room number?

350 - 2
There's nothing here.

350 - 3
Our cat had kittens.

350 - 4
Today is a holiday.

350 - 5
Show your solutions.

350 - 6
My sister is kind.

350 - 7
Do you sell swimsuits?

Day 350

Week 51

351 - 1

Let's go slowly.
Ni iru malrapide.

351 - 2

He fulfilled my needs.
Li plenumis miajn bezonojn.

351 - 3

She is bleeding.
Ŝi sangas.

351 - 4

It's eleven o'clock.
Estas la dekunua.

351 - 5

He is not available.
Li ne estas disponebla.

351 - 6

Open for residents.
Malfermita por loĝantoj.

351 - 7

Put on your slippers!
Surmetu viajn pantoflojn!

Day 351

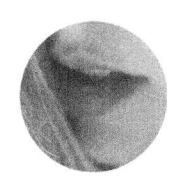

Week 51

352 - 1
Which is your bag?
Kiu estas via sako?

352 - 2
Whose mistake is it?
Kies eraro ĝi estas?

352 - 3
I have been mugged.
Oni atakis min.

352 - 4
He often watches movies.
Li ofte spektas filmojn.

352 - 5
Stay with me.
Restu kun mi.

352 - 6
I feel guilty.
Mi sentas min kulpa.

352 - 7
Sorry but we are full.
Pardonu sed ni estas plenaj.

Day 352

Week 51

353 - 1

I really enjoyed it.
Mi tre ĝuis ĝin.

353 - 2

Don't disturb me.
Ne ĝenu min.

353 - 3

He said in a low voice.
Li diris mallaŭte.

353 - 4

There's a book here.
Estas libro ĉi tie.

353 - 5

I want to get in shape.
Mi volas esti en formo.

353 - 6

He's a fine man.
Li estas bona homo.

353 - 7

My aunt lives in madrid.
Mia onklino loĝas en madrido.

Day 353

Week 51

354 - 1

Drink plenty of water.
Trinku multe da akvo.

354 - 2

What did you buy?
Kion vi aĉetis?

354 - 3

It is a heart attack.
Ĝi estas koratako.

354 - 4

When is the next train?
Kiam estas la sekva trajno?

354 - 5

I love tomatoes.
Mi amas tomatojn.

354 - 6

What can you say?
Kion vi povas diri?

354 - 7

Both are the same.
Ambaŭ estas samaj.

Day 354

Week 51

355 - 1

Are you ok?
Ĉu vi bonfartas?

355 - 2

Before you begin.
Antaŭ ol vi komencos.

355 - 3

Whatever you want.
Kion ajn vi volas.

355 - 4

I didn't do it.
Mi ne faris ĝin.

355 - 5

I couldn't care less.
Mi ne povus zorgi malpli.

355 - 6

Let's call the waiter.
Ni voku la kelneron.

355 - 7

Dry your hair well.
Sekigu viajn harojn bone.

Day 355

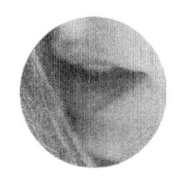

Week 51

356 - 1

It's okay.
Estas bone.

356 - 2

His wife is beautiful.
Lia edzino estas bela.

356 - 3

You should read a lot.
Vi devus legi multe.

356 - 4

He was shivering.
Li tremis.

356 - 5

First, you.
Unue vi.

356 - 6

Good morning, teacher.
Bonan matenon, instruisto.

356 - 7

Wonderful, thank you.
Mirinde, dankon.

Day 356

Test 51

357 - 1
Open for residents.

357 - 2
Stay with me.

357 - 3
There's a book here.

357 - 4
It is a heart attack.

357 - 5
Before you begin.

357 - 6
It's okay.

357 - 7
Wonderful, thank you.

Day 357

Week 52

358 - 1

He looked at me.
Li rigardis min.

358 - 2

I love to eat.
Mi amas manĝi.

358 - 3

Do not iron.
Ne gladu.

358 - 4

I feel sick today.
Mi sentas min malsana hodiaŭ.

358 - 5

Never mind.
Ne gravas.

358 - 6

Yes, i'd love to.
Jes, mi ŝatus.

358 - 7

He stood on the stage.
Li staris sur la scenejo.

Day 358

Week 52

359 - 1

Be aware of cyclists.
Estu konscia pri biciklantoj.

359 - 2

What do you recommend?
Kion vi rekomendas?

359 - 3

The air is clean here.
La aero estas pura ĉi tie.

359 - 4

May i use your computer?
Ĉu mi rajtas uzi vian komputilon?

359 - 5

That sounds delicious!
Tio sonas bongusta!

359 - 6

Next is your turn.
Poste estas via vico.

359 - 7

My shirt is ripped up.
Mia ĉemizo estas ŝirita.

Day 359

Week 52

Please eat.
Bonvolu manĝi.

What did he ask you?
Kion li demandis al vi?

I get up at 5.15.
Mi ellitiĝas je 5.15.

Don't worry.
Ne zorgu.

She's 27 years old.
Ŝi aĝas 27 jarojn.

The sky is deep blue.
La ĉielo estas profunde blua.

I dried the wet clothes.
Mi sekigis la malsekajn vestaĵojn.

Day 360

LEARN ESPERANTO IN 52 WEEKS

LEARN ESPERANTO IN 52 WEEKS WITH 7 SENTENCES A DAY

Week 52

361 - 1

Get lost.
Foriru.

361 - 2

We have an emergency.
Ni havas krizon.

361 - 3

He spoke loudly.
Li parolis laŭte.

361 - 4

I will ask them to wait.
Mi petos ilin atendi.

361 - 5

I think you're right.
Mi pensas, ke vi pravas.

361 - 6

Oh no, what a shame.
Ho ne, kia domaĝo.

361 - 7

She talks fast.
Ŝi parolas rapide.

Day 361

Week 52

362 - 1

You're so sweet.
Vi estas tiel dolĉa.

362 - 2

I lost my key today.
Mi perdis mian ŝlosilon hodiaŭ.

362 - 3

Come again?
Revenu?

362 - 4

Clean up your place.
Purigu vian lokon.

362 - 5

Are you joking?
Ĉu vi ŝercas?

362 - 6

It's been so cold.
Estis tiel malvarme.

362 - 7

Can i leave my bag here?
Ĉu mi povas lasi mian sakon ĉi tie?

Day 362

LEARN ESPERANTO IN 52 WEEKS

LEARN ESPERANTO IN 52 WEEKS WITH 7 SENTENCES A DAY

Week 52

363 - 1

Good morning.
Bonan matenon.

363 - 2

Who designed this one?
Kiu desegnis ĉi tiun?

363 - 3

My feel hurt.
Mia sento vundita.

363 - 4

Will you meet me?
Ĉu vi renkontos min?

363 - 5

Take care of yourself.
Prizorgu vin.

363 - 6

Just a minute please.
Nur minuton bonvolu.

363 - 7

Call the nurse.
Voku la flegistinon.

Day 363

Test 52

364 - 1

Yes, i'd love to.

364 - 2

That sounds delicious!

364 - 3

Don't worry.

364 - 4

He spoke loudly.

364 - 5

I lost my key today.

364 - 6

Good morning.

364 - 7

Call the nurse.

Day 364

See you soon

Learn English in 52 weeks
Learn French in 52 weeks
Learn Bulgarian in 52 weeks
Learn Chinese in 52 weeks
Learn Czech in 52 weeks
Learn Danish in 52 weeks
Learn Dutch in 52 weeks
Learn Estonian in 52 weeks
Learn Finnish in 52 weeks
Learn German in 52 weeks
Learn Greek in 52 weeks
Learn Hungarian in 52 weeks
Learn Italian in 52 weeks
Learn Japanese in 52 weeks
Learn Latvian in 52 weeks
Learn Lithuanian in 52 weeks
Learn Polish in 52 weeks
Learn Portuguese in 52 weeks
Learn Brazilian in 52 weeks
Learn Romanian in 52 weeks
Learn Russian in 52 weeks
Learn Slovak in 52 weeks
Learn Spanish in 52 weeks
Learn Swedish in 52 weeks